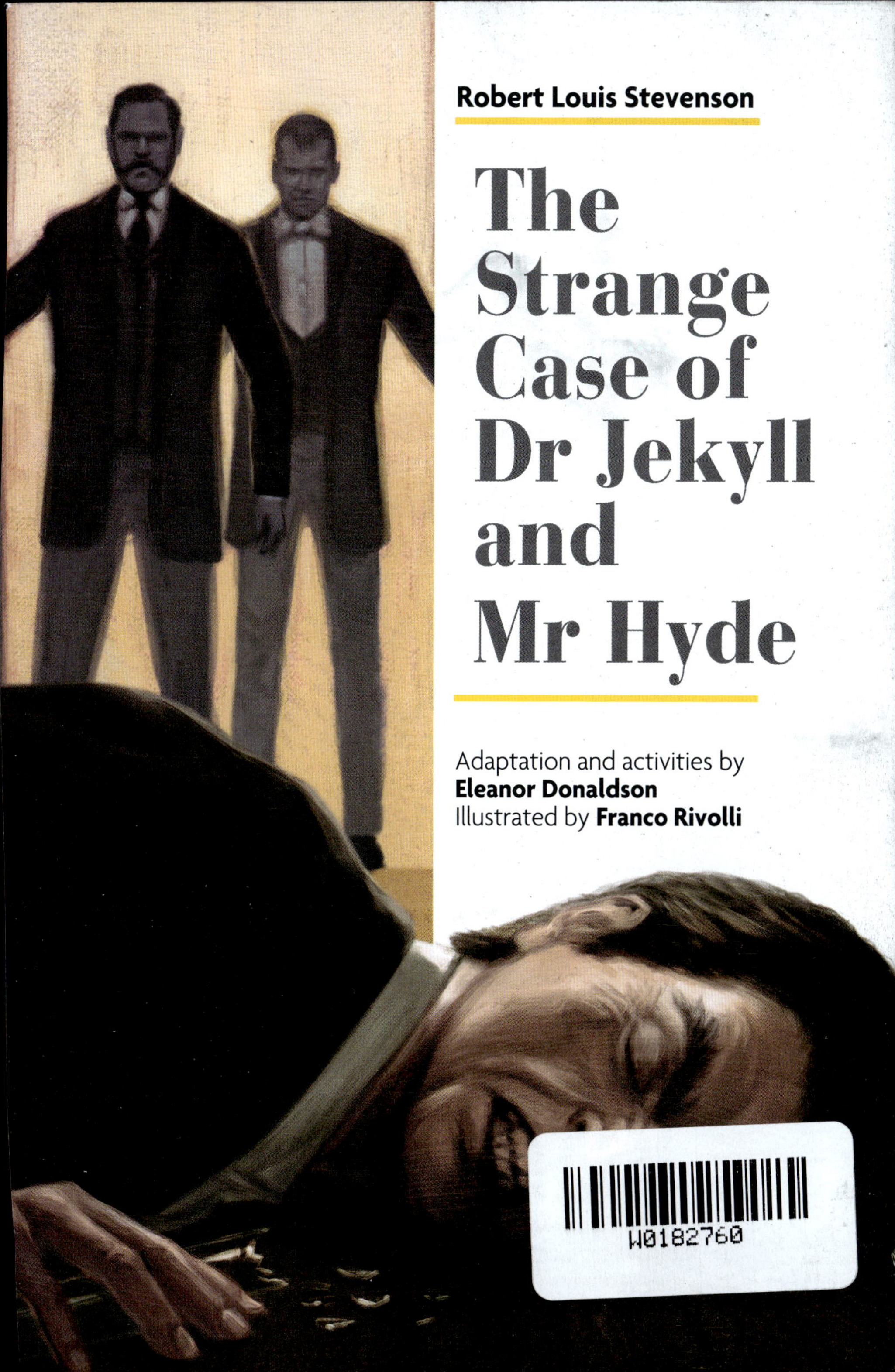

Robert Louis Stevenson

The Strange Case of Dr Jekyll and Mr Hyde

Adaptation and activities by
Eleanor Donaldson
Illustrated by **Franco Rivolli**

Member of CISQ Federation

CERTIFIED MANAGEMENT SYSTEM
ISO 9001
The design, production and distribution of educational materials for the CIDEB (Black Cat) brand are managed in compliance with the rules of Quality Management System which fulfils the requirements of the standard ISO 9001

Content editor: Maria Grazia Donati
Editor: Francesca Pinagli
Design: Erika Barabino, Silvia Bassi, Daniele Pagliari
Page Layout: Annalisa Possenti
Picture research: Alice Graziotin

Art Director: Nadia Maestri

First edition: January 2019

Picture credits:
Shutterstock; iStockphoto; Dreamstime;
Culture Club/Getty Images:4;
© Look and Learn/Bridgeman Images: 5;
Eric Farrelly/Alamy Stock Photo: 62b;
COLLECTION CHRISTOPHEL/MONDADORI PORTFOLIO: 65;
Vontica/Alamy Stock Photo: 86.

We would be happy to give you further information concerning our material and receive your comments.

info@blackcat-cideb.com
blackcat-cideb.com

Printed in Genoa, Italy, by Litoprint srl

Contents

4 **Robert Louis Stevenson**

8 **Before you read**

11 **Chapter 1 -** Mr Enfield's tale

Chapter 2 - The will 17

Chapter 3 - The murderer 24

Chapter 4 - Dr Lanyon's quarrel 31

Chapter 5 - The man in the laboratory 38

Chapter 6 - Where is Henry Jekyll? 45

Chapter 7 - Dr Lanyon's letter 51

Chapter 8 - The confession of Dr Jekyll 56

62 **Dossiers**

Deacon Brodie 62

Mad scientists and monsters: *Frankenstein* 65

67 **Activities**

n.track THE STORY IS FULLY RECORDED

Robert Louis Stevenson

Robert Louis Stevenson was a Scottish writer. As well as novels, he wrote poetry, essays, short stories and travel books.

Stevenson was born in the City of Edinburgh in the middle of the 19th century, in 1850. His father was an engineer and his grandfather and father built lighthouses.[1] His mother came from a family of lawyers and religious ministers.[2] When he was a child, he became ill with tuberculosis. His nurse,[3] Alison Cunningham, stayed with the family to look after him. She was very religious and she told him stories about heaven and hell.[4] Later, he remembered these frightening stories of good and evil.[5]

When he was seventeen, he went to university in Edinburgh. At first, he studied Engineering, like his father, but he wasn't interested in the subject so he decided to study Law instead. Although in

1. **lighthouse :** 
2. **minister :** a religious man in some Christian churches.
3. **nurse :** (here) a person who looks after children (a nanny); a person who looks after someone who is sick.
4. **heaven and hell :** in some religions, places people go when they die. Heaven is a good place and hell is bad.
5. **evil :** very bad or unpleasant (opposite of *good*).

1875 he passed an exam to become a lawyer, he never worked as a lawyer. Possibly, he always knew that he wanted to become a writer.

Sadly, Stevenson's ill health as a child meant that he had serious health problems all his life. For this reason, he left the cold, wet weather of Scotland and travelled around France and Spain. On a visit to France in 1876, he met an American woman, Fanny Osbourne. They fell in love, and Stevenson followed her to America, where they were married in 1880 in California.

After a short period of time in California, they went to Scotland and England, but in 1887, Stevenson and Fanny left the country forever. They returned first to America, and then they went to the South Pacific. Finally, they made their home on one of the islands of Samoa in 1890. There the local people called him *Tusitala*, which means 'storyteller' in the local language. Stevenson's health got better, but in 1894, he died suddenly of a brain haemorrhage.[6] He was only forty-four years old.

Although Robert Louis Stevenson wrote about many of his real-life adventures in his travel books, he is probably best known for his fiction. Stevenson always said he wanted to write exciting

▶ *Treasure Island*

6. brain haemorrhage : when the brain starts to lose a lot of blood.

stories: 'Fiction is to grown men what play is to the child,' he said. His adventure stories were famous, and younger readers still enjoy them. Examples are *Treasure Island* (1883), *Kidnapped* (1886), set in 18th-century Scotland, and *The Black Arrow* (1888), set in a time of war in 15th-century England. However, *The Strange Case of Dr Jekyll and Mr Hyde* (1886) and the book he was still finishing when he died, *Weir of Hermiston* (published in 1896), show the dark, adult side of Stevenson.

1 Comprehension Check • Complete the questions with a word from the box. Then match questions (1-8) to an answer (a-h).

job age name city illness famous books wife

1. ☐ In which .... was Stevenson born?
2. ☐ What .... did Stevenson's father do?
3. ☐ What .... did Stevenson have when he was a child?
4. ☐ Where did Stevenson first meet his .... ?
5. ☐ What does the Samoan .... *Tusitala* mean?
6. ☐ What type of writing is Stevenson most .... for?
7. ☐ As well as *The Strange Case of Dr Jekyll and Mr Hyde*, which other .... did Stevenson write?
8. ☐ What .... was Stevenson when he died?

a *Treasure Island, Kidnapped, The Black Arrow* and others
b tuberculosis
c storyteller
d fiction
e France
f forty-four years old
g engineer
h Edinburgh

2 Match the sentences to a date on the timeline.

a 1850 — **b** 1867 — **c** 1876 — **d** 1880 — **e** 1890 — **f** 1894

1. ☐ Fanny and Robert were married.
2. ☐ Robert Louis Stevenson was born in Edinburgh, Scotland.
3. ☐ Stevenson died suddenly of a brain haemorrhage.
4. ☐ Stevenson met his wife, Fanny Osborne.
5. ☐ Robert Louis Stevenson went to university.
6. ☐ They made their home on the islands of Samoa.

3 Use the question words in the box to ask and answer questions using dates in the biography.

When was ... ? When did ... ? When did he write ... ?
Who did ... meet in ... ? What happened in ... ? Where did he travel/live in ... ?

4 Stevenson travelled a lot. He wrote travel books as well as fiction. From the information in the biography, circle the names of countries that Stevenson lived in.

Scotland France USA Samoa Canada Australia Japan

5 Quiz • The sentences (1-6) contain some information about Robert Louis Stevenson, but not all of them are true. Can you guess which are true/false? Look at the answers at the bottom of the page. Are you surprised by any of the answers?

1. He wrote stories about the detective Sherlock Holmes.
2. He wrote a book about a journey from Belgium in a canoe.
3. His uncle was also a lighthouse engineer.
4. Stevenson later became known as a national poet.
5. One of Stevenson's favourite hobbies was sailing.
6. In Stevenson's book *Treasure Island*, the sailors were afraid of a 'red spot'.

Key: **1.** F – This was Sir Arthur Conan Doyle. **2.** T **3.** T **4.** F – Stevenson wrote poetry, but was not called a national poet like Robert (Rabbie) Burns. **5.** T **6.** F – It was a black spot.

BEFORE YOU READ

1 Vocabulary • Read the words in the box. Check their meaning. Tick the words you can see in the photographs.

axe ☐ poker ☐ crowd ☐ cheque book ☐ safe ☐ will ☐
stick ☐ wallet ☐ powders ☐ experiments ☐ papers ☐
apparatus ☐ test tube ☐

1

2

3

4

5

6

7

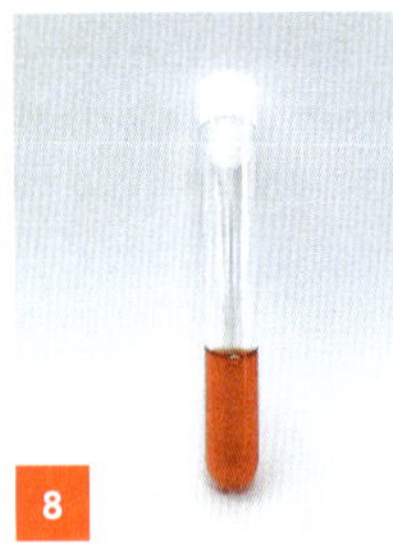
8

2 Choose the best category (1-5) for the words in the box in exercise 1. (Some words can be in more than one category.)

1. Hard objects **2.** Money **3.** Documents **4.** In the laboratory **5.** People

3 Which of these words are about crime and detection?

suspicious forgery company blackmail victim
inspector witness murder fog mystery pleasant clerk
friendship desk elegant clue confession

4 Characters • Match the words in A with a word that means the opposite in B.

A		B	
0.	[b] polite	a	in order
1.	[ ] untidy	b	rude
2.	[ ] bent	c	dreadful
3.	[ ] glad	d	ugly
4.	[ ] cruel	e	unhappy
5.	[ ] wonderful	f	caring
6.	[ ] good	g	straight
7.	[ ] pretty	h	evil

5 Look at the picture of the characters on page 10. Describe their appearance. Which person do you think looks: a) serious; b) intelligent; c) strange?

6 Titles • Look at the titles in the story (1-8). Read the sentences (a-h). Can you guess in which part of the story the events happen? Match a sentence to a title.

1. [ ] Mr Enfield's tale
2. [ ] The will
3. [ ] The murderer
4. [ ] Dr Lanyon's quarrel
5. [ ] The man in the laboratory
6. [ ] Where is Henry Jekyll?
7. [ ] Dr Lanyon's letter
8. [ ] The confession of Dr Jekyll

a A man violently attacks a well-known, important gentleman.
b The doctor's servant and the lawyer are confused by the doctor's disappearance.
c Mr Utterson, a lawyer, is confused by his friend's wish to leave his money to a terrible man.
d Once the lawyer reads his friend's story the mystery becomes clearer.
e Two doctors disagree strongly. Later, one of them becomes ill.
f Mr Utterson finally learns the truth about his client in his own words.
g Mr Utterson's cousin tells him a story about a man and a mysterious door.
h A strange person asks the servant, Poole, for powders for his experiments.

The Characters

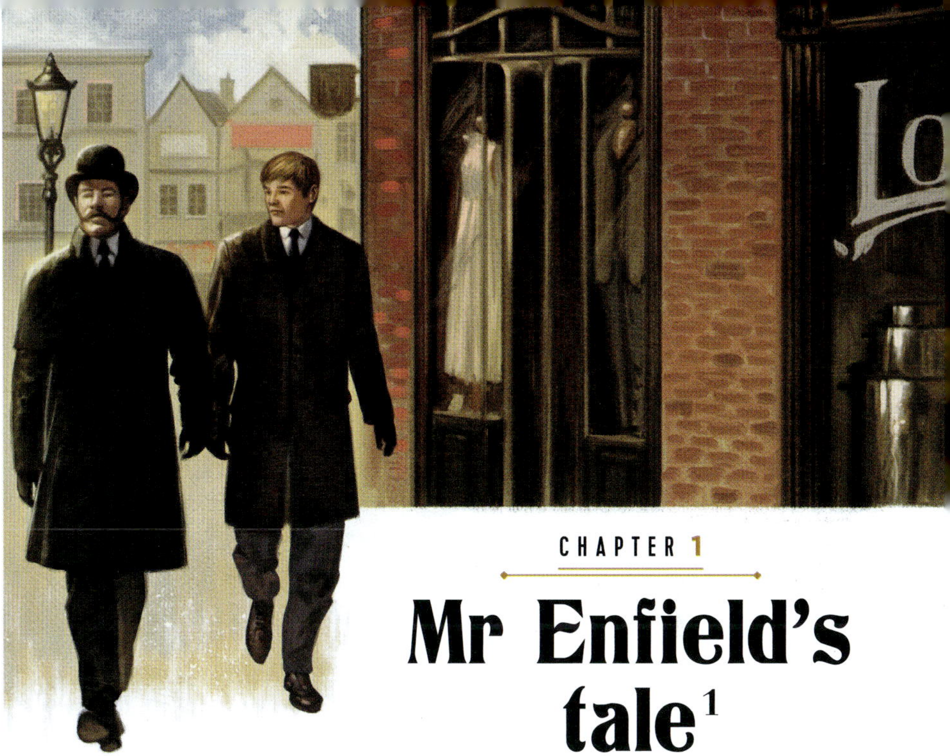

CHAPTER 1

Mr Enfield's tale[1]

Mr Utterson was known in London as a good, honest lawyer. He was a small, thin man with a serious face. Although he seemed unfriendly, those who knew him said he was caring and a good listener. When a man became his friend, they were a true friend for life and he accepted their faults[2] with patience. Mr Utterson lived a quiet life. He had enough money to buy nice things, but he was a man of simple pleasures.

track 02

One of these pleasures was to go for a walk every Sunday with his cousin and friend, Mr Richard Enfield. Many people were surprised at their friendship. They did not have many similar interests and the two men often walked in silence, smiling and nodding[3] at the people they met in the street. However, they both looked forward

1. **tale :** (here) story.
2. **faults :** the bad things in a person's character.
3. **nodding :** moving their heads up and down to greet, or agree.

to their meetings and they seemed to enjoy each other's company.

It was on one of these walks, in a quiet part of the city, that Mr Enfield told his story. The two friends were walking along a pretty, narrow side street. Every shop window seemed to have attractive displays[4] of food, clothes and objects for the home. The shops were clean and bright and the sun shone pleasantly on their painted doors. But a little further down, there stood a small, ugly building with no windows. The door was dark and dirty, and no one seemed to live there.

Mr Enfield stopped in front of the house for a moment. Then he said to Mr Utterson, 'Do you see that old house? I can tell you a story about that place.'

'Really?' said Mr Utterson. 'Tell me.'

'Well,' Mr Enfield began. 'One night I was walking home along this street. It was winter, and it was very late. There was nobody in the street. I began to feel frightened. Suddenly, I saw two people. One was a little girl, and the other was a man. The man was walking down the main street. The little girl was running along this street towards the main street. They ran into each other at the corner and the little girl fell down.

'Then something horrible happened, and I've never been able to forget it. The little girl was on the ground. The man continued walking. He walked right over the girl's body! She began to

4. displays : collections of objects for people to look at.

scream[5] and cry. The way he walked over her was very frightening. He didn't seem to care.

'I went after the man, and I brought him back. He was a small man, I remember, and there was something strange about him. I hated him the moment I saw him, but I don't know why.

'When we came back to the little girl, there was a crowd in the street. The girl's family was there. There was also a doctor. The girl was all right, but she was crying. Her family was very upset.[6] We couldn't believe what the man had done. He didn't even say sorry. Everybody was so angry. Some people said they wanted to kill him. We decided to punish[7] him.

'We told him to pay the girl's family some money. We told him to give them one hundred pounds. It was a lot of money.

'"We will tell everybody," I said. "You will have no friends when they know what you did tonight."

'The man was frightened.

'"Very well," agreed the man, "I will give the family one hundred pounds."

'It was late at night. It's difficult to find a hundred pounds in the middle of the night. We went with the man, and he came to this old house. He opened the door with a key. He went inside, and he came out with the money. He had ten pounds in notes, and a cheque for ninety pounds. The cheque was not his – it was signed by another man. This other man is very well known in London.

'"This is very strange," I thought. "Perhaps the cheque is a forgery."

'I told the horrible man my suspicions.[8] He laughed at me.

'"If you don't trust me," he said, "I'll stay with you until the bank opens."

5. scream : make a loud, high noise of pain and/or fear.
6. upset : unhappy or worried because something unpleasant has happened.
7. punish : do something to someone who has done something wrong.
8. suspicions : (here) thoughts that the cheque was not real.

'So the man stayed with us, and in the morning we all went to the bank. The bank paid the cheque – it was not a forgery, after all.'

'Oh!' said Mr Utterson sadly.

'I know what you're thinking,' Mr Enfield said. 'If the man who wrote the cheque is a good man, why would he want to be a friend of this dreadful man? Perhaps the man who hurt the girl is blackmailing him.'

Mr Utterson looked at the house again.

'The man who wrote the cheque,' he asked his friend, 'does he live in that house?'

'No,' said Mr Enfield, 'he doesn't live there. I discovered that later. He lives somewhere else.'

'So who actually lives in the house?' Mr Utterson asked.

'I don't know,' Mr Enfield said. 'I didn't want to ask too many questions. I don't like asking questions. But I know that the strange man uses the house very often. I have seen him come in and go out.'

Mr Utterson was silent for a moment. Then he said, 'I agree with you: it is best not to ask questions sometimes. But tell me, do you know the name of the strange man you saw that night?'

'Yes,' answered Mr Enfield. 'His name is Mr Hyde.'

'What is he like?' asked Mr Utterson.

'He is small,' said Mr Enfield, 'and there is something ugly about him. Like I said, I hated him the moment I saw him.'

'You say that he had a key to the door of this house?' asked Mr Utterson.

'Yes, he did,' Mr Enfield replied. 'He opened the door with a key.'

Mr Utterson looked sad again. Then he said, 'I haven't asked you about the man who wrote the cheque. That is because I believe that I already know his name.'

THINK!

Use a dictionary to find new words in the box. Which of these words are 'qualities'? Underline Mr Utterson's qualities. Would you trust him?

arrogant cold fair caring patient honest brave cruel irresponsible trustworthy

Have you ever met someone you didn't like? How do you feel about Mr Hyde after reading Chapter 1?

The text and beyond • page 68
Values & Feelings • page 94

CHAPTER 2

The will

The evening of his walk with Mr Enfield, Mr Utterson thought unhappily about his friend's tale. Although he ate dinner, he did not feel hungry. Something was worrying him. Instead of passing the evening in front of the fire with a good book as he usually did, he went to the desk in his office. There, he took out a document from a locked[1] drawer. He examined it carefully.

track 03

The document was the will of a client[2] and his friend, Dr Jekyll. It was written by Dr Jekyll himself. Mr Utterson was not happy about the will, but he had followed his client's orders. The details of the will were these: Dr Jekyll was going to leave all his money to his friend, 'Mr Edward Hyde'. But there was another part of the will

1. locked : closed with a key.
2. client : someone who pays for his services.

that worried Mr Utterson. If Dr Jekyll disappeared for more than three months or went away, then Mr Hyde could have all his money.

As a lawyer, Mr Utterson found the will confusing. He didn't always agree with Dr Jekyll, but his friend was a good man. He did not understand why his friend was going to leave all his money to this young man. Now Mr Utterson had heard Mr Enfield's story, his worst fears were confirmed.[3] Mr Hyde was not a nice man, in fact he was a terrible man. And what did Jekyll mean by 'disappearance'? It was all very strange. 'There's a secret here,' he thought, 'and I need to know the truth.'

He decided to visit their old friend, Dr Lanyon.

'If anyone can help, it is Dr Lanyon,' he said to himself.

Dr Lanyon was happy to see Mr Utterson. They talked together for a while.[4] Then Mr Utterson said, 'We have all been friends for a long time. You and I are Dr Jekyll's oldest friends, I suppose?'

'I suppose we are,' Dr Lanyon agreed. 'But I don't see Jekyll often these days.'

'Oh?' said Mr Utterson. 'I thought you had the same interests.'

'No!' replied Dr Lanyon angrily. 'Not now. We used to have similar interests, but I don't like Henry Jekyll's ideas about science. He has such strange ideas!'

---

3. confirmed : showed that they must be true.
4. for a while : for a short period of time.

'Tell me,' said Mr Utterson, 'do you know a man called Hyde?'

Dr Lanyon thought for a moment.

'Hyde?' he asked. 'No, I don't know the name.'

Mr Utterson returned home after his visit to Dr Lanyon. He could not sleep that night. He was worried about his friend. He remembered Mr Enfield's story about Mr Hyde and the little girl.

'I want to see this Mr Hyde!' he decided. 'I want to understand more about his friendship with Henry Jekyll.'

Mr Utterson went back to the old house often now. He waited in the street, where he hoped to see Mr Hyde. He went there every day for three weeks, but Mr Hyde didn't come.

Then, one night, Mr Utterson was near the old house when he heard someone in the street. He saw a man walking towards the house. Mr Utterson followed him to the door, and then he spoke to him.

'Are you Mr Hyde?' he asked.

The man seemed frightened for a moment. Then he looked at Mr Utterson angrily.

'I am Mr Hyde. What do you want?'

'I see that you're going into this house,' said Mr Utterson. 'I'm a friend of Dr Jekyll – perhaps you will ask me into the house?'

'Dr Jekyll is not at home,' Mr Hyde said.

'I am glad we have met,' Mr Utterson said. 'I shall recognise you again. It may be useful.'

'I am glad we have met, too,' said Mr Hyde. He gave Mr Utterson a piece of paper with his address written on it.

'He's thinking of the will,' Mr Utterson thought. 'He's glad we met because of the will! That's why he wants me to know where he lives.'

Mr Hyde entered the house and closed the door behind him.

'I don't like that man!' thought Mr Utterson. 'There's something very strange about him. Poor Henry, why have you got a friend like that?'

The lawyer walked to the end of the street and turned the corner. The houses there were large, but the inhabitants did not appear to take care of them. Some of them had broken doors and windows. However, one house further down the street was different to the others. It looked comfortable, welcoming and wealthy. Mr Utterson stopped at this house and knocked. A servant opened the door.

'Good evening, Poole,' Mr Utterson said. 'I am looking for Dr Jekyll. Is he at home?'

'Please come in, sir,' the servant said. 'I will see if Dr Jekyll is at home.'

Poole came back after a few moments.

'I'm sorry, sir,' he told Mr Utterson. 'Dr Jekyll has gone out.'

'I saw Mr Hyde go into the laboratory at the back of the house,' said Mr Utterson.

'Does he often come when Dr Jekyll is out?'

'Yes, sir,' Poole answered. 'Mr Hyde has a key to the laboratory.'

'Are Dr Jekyll and Mr Hyde good friends?' asked the lawyer.

'They are very good friends, sir,' Poole said. 'We have orders to obey Mr Hyde[5] when he comes to the laboratory.'

'I have never met Mr Hyde at dinner here,' the lawyer said.

'No, sir,' Poole agreed. 'Mr Hyde never dines here. He never comes to this part of the house. He stays in the laboratory.'

Mr Utterson thanked the servant and left the house. He felt very upset.

'Poor Henry Jekyll!' he thought. 'He lived badly[6] when he was a young man. Mr Hyde must know some secret from the past. My friend is paying him to be quiet about the secret. My poor, poor friend – I'll help him if I can!'

Two weeks later, Dr Jekyll invited some of his friends to dinner at his house. Mr Utterson was one of the guests. After the other guests had gone, Mr Utterson stayed to talk with his friend.

'I want to talk to you about something important,' the lawyer said. 'It concerns your will, Jekyll.'

'I know what you want to say, my friend,' Dr Jekyll told him. 'I know you're not happy about my will, but you shouldn't worry about it.'

'I know some things about Mr Hyde,' Utterson said quietly. 'People say dreadful things about him.'

5. obey Mr Hyde : do what Mr Hyde says.
6. lived badly : did some bad things.

'You do not understand,' Dr Jekyll said. 'You do not understand my position. It's very difficult for me –'

'Jekyll!' the lawyer interrupted him. 'You know me. We're old friends. If you're in trouble, tell me the truth. Perhaps I can help you.'

'You're a good friend, Utterson,' Dr Jekyll said. 'Thank you for your offer of help. But you cannot help me. I know you have seen Mr Hyde – he told me. I can't tell you any more about this, but I trust you to follow the orders in my will. Promise me that you will follow them.'

'I will never like Mr Hyde,' the lawyer said.

'I don't ask that,' Dr Jekyll told his friend. 'I ask only that you help him when I am not here.'

'Very well,' the lawyer said. 'I will do what you want.'

THINK!

Think about Mr Utterson's feelings when he remembers Dr Jekyll's decision to leave his money to Mr Hyde. Using the information in Chapter 2, read the sentences and tick two sentences that are true.

1 ☐ He doesn't care. His client can make his own decisions.
2 ☐ He is confused about why Dr Jekyll wants to be friends with Mr Hyde.
3 ☐ He is worried that his friend is in trouble and he wants to help him.
4 ☐ He is happy that Dr Jekyll knows what he is doing.

Think about the value of honesty. Which of these actions is honest?

1 ☐ To keep secrets because someone trusts you not to tell them.
2 ☐ To tell someone the truth when they ask you for the facts.
3 ☐ To ask someone to believe you.

Has anyone asked you to make a promise to them? Could you keep this promise? When might you break a promise?

The text and beyond • page 70
Values & Feelings • page 94

CHAPTER 3

The murderer

Nearly a year had passed since Mr Utterson's conversation with Dr Jekyll. One night, a thick fog fell across the city. A young servant girl was staring[1] dreamily[2] from her bedroom window. The full moon shone brightly through the fog on the street below. Although the servant girl could only remember a few details of what happened next, what she remembered was both frightening and surprising. The attack she witnessed was very violent. Indeed,[3] it was even more shocking because the victim was a well-known, important man. Soon everyone in London was talking about the news of a terrible murder. This is how she described the events.

track 04

1. **staring :** looking at; fixed her eye on.
2. **dreamily :** thinking about pleasant things.
3. **Indeed :** (formal) In fact.

She had gone to bed at about eleven o'clock. She could not sleep so she got out of bed and went to sit by the window. She saw an old man who was walking along the street. The old man had white hair. She also saw another, small man, walking towards the old man. When the two men met, the old man said something to the small man. He seemed to be asking a question. The girl could not hear the words he spoke, but she said that he spoke very politely. Then the girl recognised the small man. It was Mr Hyde. She knew him because he sometimes came to the house where she worked, to speak to her employer.

Mr Hyde was carrying a heavy stick in his hand. He did not answer the old man's question. Suddenly, he lifted his stick above his head and began to hit the old man with it. He hit him again and again, and the old man fell to the ground. Then Mr Hyde attacked him where he lay on the ground. The girl was horrified at the violence of the attack, and she fainted.[4]

It was two o'clock in the morning when the girl woke up from her faint. She called the police immediately. The murderer had gone, but the old man was lying in the street. The police found a piece of the

4. fainted : became unconscious.

murderer's stick in the street next to the old man's body. When they searched the body,[5] they also found the old man's wallet and papers, and a letter. The letter was addressed to his lawyer, Mr Utterson.

The police came to Mr Utterson's house early the next morning. He became very serious when they told him about the murder.

'I want to see the body,' he said. 'I can say nothing until I have seen the body.'

Mr Utterson went to the police station where the police had carried the body.

'Yes,' said Mr Utterson, 'I recognise this man. It is Sir Danvers Carew. He is a client of mine and a Member of Parliament.'

'Sir Danvers Carew!' the policeman said. 'Goodness me! Is it possible?' He looked at Mr Utterson.

'When the newspapers know of this, everyone will be talking about it,' he said. 'Perhaps you can help us find this man, Mr Utterson.'

The policeman told Mr Utterson what the girl had seen. Mr Utterson was unhappy when he heard the name of Hyde. He asked to look at the piece of the murderer's stick. He recognised it immediately.

'This Mr Hyde,' he asked the policeman. 'Does the girl say that he was a small man?'

'She says that he is a small, ugly man,' the policeman said.

5. **searched the body :** looked for things in the dead man's clothes.

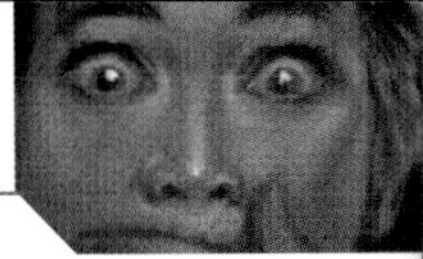

Mr Utterson thought for a moment about the piece of paper Mr Hyde had given him with his address. 'Come with me,' he said. 'I think I know where he lives.'

Mr Utterson and the policeman went to the part of the city where Mr Hyde lived. It was a dirty, poor part of the city. The wind blew hard and cold. The sun had risen, but it was still dark. The orange light of the dawn sky broke through the clouds like a fire in the yellowish-grey of the early morning fog.

They knocked on the door of Mr Hyde's house. An old woman with an evil face opened the door. She told them that Mr Hyde was out. She explained that Mr Hyde had come in very late the night before. Then he had gone out again.

'We want to search his rooms,' the lawyer said. 'This man is Inspector Newcomen of Scotland Yard.'

'What has Mr Hyde done?' the old woman asked. 'Why are the police looking for him?'

The old woman showed the two men Mr Hyde's rooms. They were comfortable rooms, with elegant furniture and pictures. The rooms were untidy, however. They found clothes on the floor, and part of Mr Hyde's stick behind the door. There was also part of a cheque book in the fireplace. Someone had tried to burn it.

Mr Utterson and the inspector went to the bank. They discovered that Mr Hyde's bank account contained thousands of pounds.

'We will find him, sir,' the inspector told Mr Utterson. 'He cannot escape the police. We have the evidence we need. We can prove that

he is the murderer. We have his stick, and we know where his bank is. We will wait for him to go to the bank. We will put up pictures of him all over the city.'

It was not easy to find pictures of Mr Hyde. He had no family, and he had no friends. There was no photograph of him anywhere. The people who had seen him could not describe him. Everybody agreed that he was small and ugly – but no one could describe him accurately.

It was late in the afternoon when Mr Utterson arrived at Dr Jekyll's house. The servant Poole took the lawyer through the main part of the house to the laboratory. It was the first time that Mr Utterson had been to Dr Jekyll's laboratory. He looked at the scientific apparatus with curiosity.

'Have you heard the terrible news?' he asked his friend.

Dr Jekyll looked very unhappy.

'Yes,' he said, 'everybody is talking about this murder.'

'Listen to me,' said the lawyer slowly. 'Carew was my client. You are also my client. I want to understand exactly what has happened. Are you hiding Mr Hyde?'

'I will never see Hyde again!' the doctor cried. 'I promise you, my friend, I have finished with that man. But he doesn't need my help. He has gone, and no one will find him.'

'You seem very certain,' Mr Utterson said.

'I am certain,' Dr Jekyll told him. 'No one will see Hyde again. But there is something else. I need your advice. I have received a letter, and I don't know what to do with it. Will you advise me?'

'Show me this letter,' the lawyer said.

Dr Jekyll gave the lawyer a letter. It was written by Edward Hyde. In his letter Mr Hyde thanked Dr Jekyll for his friendship.

He said that he was sorry for what he had done, and that he was going away.

'Where is the envelope?' asked Mr Utterson.

'I burnt the envelope,' Dr Jekyll told him, 'but the letter was not posted. Someone came to the house and left it here.'

'I shall think about the letter,' Mr Utterson said. 'One other thing. Was it Mr Hyde who made you write the will?'

Dr Jekyll looked at his friend. He said nothing, but he nodded his head.

'I thought it was him!' the lawyer cried. 'He planned to murder you. He wanted your money.'

When he was leaving the house, Mr Utterson spoke to Poole for a moment.

'Someone came with a letter for Dr Jekyll today,' he said. 'What did the man look like?'

'No one came with a letter, sir,' the servant told him.

'Are you sure that no one came to the house?'

Poole said he was certain. Mr Utterson thanked the servant and left.

THINK!

Choose logical words from the box to complete the newspaper article about the murder in Chapter 3. Describe your feelings after reading about the murder.

good violent shocked interesting frightening
surprised curiosity trustworthy

The Member of Parliament Sir Danvers Carew was murdered today near his home in central London. His maid, who witnessed the attack, said that she was **(1)**.................... and **(2)**.................... by the attack. 'It was **(3)**....................,' she said. 'The man hit Sir Danvers and he wouldn't stop.' Mr Hyde is described as a very **(4)**.................... man. Anyone who has information about him should report it to the police immediately.

Find the word *secretive* in a dictionary. Who keeps secrets in Chapter 3? Who tells the truth?

The text and beyond • page 72
Values & Feelings • page 94

CHAPTER 4

Dr Lanyon's quarrel

Mr Utterson was still thinking about the letter when he returned home. Maybe the person had left the letter at the laboratory at the back of the house. That was the reason why the servant, Poole, hadn't seen anyone.

track 05

The lawyer knew he must be careful. The murder was still on the front pages of all the newspapers. He needed someone he could trust. Fortunately, he knew a man who could help.

That evening, he was sitting by the fire with his friend and head clerk,[1] Mr Guest.

'The murder of Sir Danvers Carew is very sad,' the lawyer began.

'It is, indeed,' Mr Guest agreed. 'It is terrible. The man who killed him must be mad.'

1. **head clerk :** Mr Guest manages the business and money of Mr Utterson.

CHAPTER 4

'You are an expert on crime and detection,' Mr Utterson said. 'I have a letter from Mr Hyde. Please look at it and tell me about the writer of the letter. Do you think he's really mad?'

Mr Utterson took out Mr Hyde's letter and passed it to Mr Guest.

Mr Guest studied the letter for a few minutes. Then he said, 'Well, sir, the writer of this letter is not mad. But his writing is strange. I know this writing, I am sure I do.'

Mr Guest picked up a letter from Dr Jekyll. He put it next to the letter from Mr Hyde.

'I thought so!' he cried. 'The same man wrote these two letters – I am sure of it.'

'I don't think we should talk about this to anyone,' Mr Utterson said.

'No, sir,' Mr Guest agreed. 'I understand.'

When he was alone again, Mr Utterson put the letter from Mr Hyde into his safe. He was very unhappy.

'Henry Jekyll forged a letter for a murderer!' he thought. 'What have you done, my old friend? And why are you protecting Hyde?'

The weeks passed and still Mr Hyde was nowhere to be found. It seemed that he had left his flat in central London and had disappeared into the night. There were more and more tales of his

wicked[2] behaviour. People spoke of his cruelty[3] and the bad people he knew. Thousands of pounds were offered to find the murderer of Sir Danvers Carew, but no one could give any details about his life or where he was now. Mr Utterson, on the other hand, felt strangely glad that Mr Hyde was gone. Maybe now a new life could begin for Dr Jekyll.

For the next two months, Dr Jekyll was much happier. He seemed cheerful and contented. He invited people to his house again and he saw his friends nearly every day. On the eighth of January, Mr Utterson had dinner at Dr Jekyll's house. Dr

2. wicked : evil, very bad.
3. cruelty : very unkind; making others feel pain or sadness.

Lanyon was there, too. The three men looked at each other with a smile.

'It was just like old times,' the lawyer thought. Then on the twelfth of January, Mr Utterson called at his friend's house again.

Poole opened the door and said, 'The doctor is at home, but he cannot see anyone. He is ill.'

Mr Utterson came back the next day, but again he could not see Jekyll. He began to worry that something had happened. He decided to visit Dr Lanyon.

Mr Utterson was shocked when he saw Dr Lanyon. The doctor looked very ill. He was white and very thin.

'The man looks like he is dying,' Mr Utterson thought. 'He is a doctor. Maybe he knows he is dying. What a horrible thought!'

'I have had a terrible shock,' Dr Lanyon told him. 'I shall never be well again. I have had a pleasant life, but everything comes to an end. I will be dead in a few weeks.'

'How sad!' thought his friend.

'Jekyll is ill, too,' Mr Utterson told him. 'I have been to his house, but Poole says he is ill. Have you seen him?'

Dr Lanyon's face changed. 'I will not speak about that man!' he said. 'I do not want you to speak about that man to me. Never mention[4] his name to me again. To me, Jekyll is a dead man!'

'We have all been friends for a long time,' the lawyer said. 'Can we do nothing for Jekyll?'

'We can do nothing for him,' Dr Lanyon said. 'Ask him yourself.'

'He won't see me,' Mr Utterson said.

Dr Lanyon looked at the lawyer very seriously.

'When I am dead, Utterson,' he said, 'you may learn the truth of

4. mention : say.

this matter.[5] I cannot tell you now. Please don't talk to me any more about Jekyll.'

When Mr Utterson got home, he wrote a letter to Dr Jekyll. He asked what was wrong with his friend, and he asked him why he had quarrelled[6] with Dr Lanyon.

The next day he received a reply from Dr Jekyll. In his letter, the doctor told him that he had decided not to see anyone in the future. He said that he could not explain the quarrel with Dr Lanyon. 'You must allow me to be alone,' he wrote. 'I have done a terrible thing, and this is my punishment.'

Mr Utterson did not understand Dr Jekyll's letter. Surely his friend was safe, now that Mr Hyde was gone? Why did he talk about 'a terrible thing' and 'punishment'? Mr Utterson began to think his friend was mad.

Dr Lanyon died about three weeks later, and Mr Utterson went to the funeral.[7] He was sad at the loss of his old friend. The night after the funeral, Mr Utterson received a large envelope. The writing was Dr Lanyon's. It said:

PRIVATE
For Mr Utterson

The lawyer opened the envelope. It contained a second envelope. The writing on the second envelope said:

Open after the death or disappearance of Dr Henry Jekyll.

'Disappearance?' thought Mr Utterson. 'What does that mean?'

5. matter : (here) situation.
6. quarrelled : argued; was angry because he didn't agree.
7. funeral : when people bury a dead person.

Then he remembered the words of Dr Jekyll's will. There was something about 'disappearance' in the will, as well.

Mr Utterson wanted to open the mysterious letter, to discover the truth. But he was a lawyer, and he decided to obey Dr Lanyon's instructions. He put the letter in his safe.

Mr Utterson went to Dr Jekyll's several times, but he never succeeded in seeing Dr Jekyll. Poole always told him the same thing: 'The doctor is in the laboratory, sir. He will not see anyone.'

It seemed that the doctor spent most of his time in the laboratory now. He slept there sometimes, according to Poole.

Soon Mr Utterson stopped going to his friend's house. It was useless. Dr Jekyll did not want to see him.

THINK!

Think of the value of friendship and answer the questions.

1 What is important to you in a friendship?
2 Do friends argue sometimes? Is this a good thing?
3 Are the following people (a, b and c) good friends?

a Dr Lanyon and Dr Jekyll
b Dr Lanyon and Mr Utterson
c Dr Jekyll and Mr Hyde

Read the sentence from Chapter 4. Choose the best answer, a, b, c or d, to describe why Mr Utterson felt like this.

'Mr Utterson, on the other hand, felt strangely glad that Mr Hyde was gone.'

a ☐ If Mr Hyde wasn't there, his friend was happier and so was he.
b ☐ If no one knew where Mr Hyde was, then he couldn't hurt his friend.
c ☐ He hated Mr Hyde. He wished the police would arrest him.
d ☐ He didn't care about the people Mr Hyde had hurt.

Think about the value of loyalty. Is Mr Utterson too loyal to Dr Jekyll?

The text and beyond • page 74
Values & Feelings • page 94

CHAPTER 5

The man in the laboratory

One Sunday afternoon, Mr Utterson was walking in the neighbourhood with Mr Enfield, as usual. They came to the street of the old house again and stopped by its door.

'I guess that is the end of the story. I don't think we will see Mr Hyde again,' Mr Enfield said.

'I hope it is,' Mr Utterson replied. 'I would rather not see Mr Hyde again. But did I ever tell you that I once saw him? It was after you told me the story about the incident you witnessed. I saw him in the street outside the door. You remember that you said you hated him when you saw him? I had the same feeling myself.'

'Everybody who saw Hyde hated him,' Mr Enfield agreed. 'But you never told me that this old house is Dr Jekyll's laboratory – I discovered that later.'

'So, you know that the entrance to the laboratory is the back of Dr Jekyll's house, do you?' said the lawyer.

Mr Enfield nodded.

'Well, in that case, you know all there is to know. Listen! I'm worried about Jekyll. Let's have a look and see if he's at home.'

The two men entered the garden of the house. They looked up and they saw Dr Jekyll. He was sitting at one of the windows. Mr Utterson walked forward.

'Jekyll!' he cried. 'I hope you are better.'

'I'm not well,' the doctor told him. 'I will die soon, I'm sure I will.'

'You need fresh air, my friend,' Mr Utterson said. 'You should come out for a walk with us. It will do you good.'

'I would like to, really I would,' Dr Jekyll said, 'but it's impossible. I am pleased to see you, Utterson. I wish I could ask you into the house to sit with me, but I can't. The house is untidy.'

'We'll stay and talk to you from here,' Mr Utterson told him. 'I was going to suggest that myself.'

'That would make me happy,' said Dr Jekyll with a smile.

But as soon as the doctor spoke these words, his face changed. The smile of welcome disappeared, and an expression of horror

came over his face. Mr Utterson saw the change in his friend's face – and then Dr Jekyll closed the window with a bang. Mr Utterson and Mr Enfield walked away from the house. They did not speak for a while.

Mr Utterson could not forget the look on Dr Jekyll's face before he closed the window. He saw it only for a brief[1] moment, but it was enough. The lawyer felt cold at the thought of it. It seemed that Mr Enfield understood because when they arrived in a busier part of the city, the two men turned towards each other.

'God forgive us!' said Mr Utterson. Mr Enfield nodded seriously. The two men did not say another word until they said goodbye.

One evening, Mr Utterson was sitting quietly at home by the fire. There was a knock at the door. He was surprised to see that it was Dr Jekyll's servant.

'Good evening, Poole,' the lawyer said. 'What can I do for you?' He looked at the servant for a moment. Poole looked pale and very frightened. 'What's the matter?' asked Mr Utterson.

1. **brief :** short.

'Mr Utterson,' Poole said, 'there is something wrong at Dr Jekyll's house. I am very worried.'

Mr Utterson gave the man a glass of water. 'Drink this,' he ordered. 'Explain everything to me. And try to stay calm.'

'I think something has happened to the doctor,' Poole said.

'Something has happened to Dr Jekyll? What do you mean?' asked Mr Utterson.

'I can't describe it. If you are able to come to the house, sir,' Poole said, 'then you can see for yourself.'

Mr Utterson walked to Dr Jekyll's house with the servant. It was a cold, March night. The wind was strong. The streets were empty, and Mr Utterson was nervous. He was sure something bad had happened. The two men reached[2] the house. Poole knocked on the door. Another servant opened the door, and Mr Utterson entered the house. All Dr Jekyll's servants were standing in the hall – they looked frightened. When she saw Mr Utterson, one of the servant girls began to cry.

'Oh, thank goodness!' she cried.

'Be quiet!' Poole said angrily. He looked tired and anxious. Then he turned to Mr Utterson.

'I'm sorry, sir, they're all afraid,' he explained. 'Will you come with me, sir? I want you to hear something. We will need to be very quiet.'

The servant led Mr Utterson[3] through the house to the laboratory. Then he spoke again.

'If Dr Jekyll asks you to come into the laboratory, you must not go in.' Poole knocked nervously on the door of the laboratory, and called out, 'Mr Utterson is here, Dr Jekyll – he wants to see you, sir.'

2. reached : arrived at.
3. led Mr Utterson : walked in front of him to show him the way.

A voice answered from inside the laboratory. 'Tell him I cannot see anyone.'

'Thank you, sir,' replied Poole. He looked at Utterson. They returned to the main part of the house.

When they arrived, he asked the lawyer, 'Now, Mr Utterson, tell me. Did that voice sound like Dr Jekyll?'

'His voice is different, certainly,' Mr Utterson admitted.

'Different!' repeated Poole. 'I have known Dr Jekyll for twenty years, and I tell you, sir, that wasn't his voice. Dr Jekyll was murdered eight days ago. I heard it myself – there was a terrible cry from that room. But who is in the room now, and why he stays there, I don't know.'

'This makes no sense, Poole,' Mr Utterson said. 'Why should anyone kill Dr Jekyll, and stay in the same room with the body? It doesn't seem right. You must be mistaken.'

'There is more, sir,' said the servant. 'Every day for a week, the person in the laboratory has left notes for me to go to the chemist to buy some kind of medicine. Every day there are more notes. I have gone to every chemist in the city. There is always something wrong with the medicine.'

'Show me one of these notes,' Mr Utterson ordered. Poole took a letter out of his pocket and gave it to Mr Utterson. The note said:

> Dr Jekyll presents his compliments[4] to Maw the chemist's. The sample[5] you sent me is useless. Dr Jekyll needs a sample of the highest quality, like the one he bought from you in the year 18—. Please send this immediately. I'm desperate – send me some of the good kind!

4. presents his compliments : a very formal way to begin a letter.
5. sample : (here) kind of medicine.

'I have seen the way Dr Jekyll writes,' Mr Utterson said. 'This seems to be the doctor's writing. Do you agree?'

'I don't know, sir,' Poole said. 'Writing isn't important – I've seen him! I've seen him, I tell you! I came to the laboratory door one day, and the door was open. I saw a man outside the laboratory. The man's face was covered. When he saw me, he ran back into the laboratory and closed the door. I swear[6] on my life. That man was not Dr Jekyll!'

6. swear : promise it is true.

THINK!

Choose words from the box to describe themes from Chapter 5.

curiosity revenge cruelty ambition determination fear loneliness care justice

Why are people interested in other people's lives? Think about these people. Do they care about Dr Jekyll or are they just curious?

1 Poole **2** Mr Utterson **3** Mr Enfield

Has someone you know ever behaved strangely? Describe the situation. How did you feel?

The text and beyond • page 76
Values & Feelings • page 94

CHAPTER 6

Where is Henry Jekyll?

track 07

Utterson thought for a moment. He tried to make sense of the servant's account.

'You can't be sure it was not your master, Poole,' the lawyer told him finally. 'I think your master is ill. Perhaps this illness has changed the doctor's face – that's why he needs the medicine.'

'No, sir,' said Poole firmly. 'The "thing" I saw in that room was not my master. I know my master. I have served him for many years. He is a fine, tall man – and the man I saw outside the laboratory was small and his back was bent[1] and twisted.'[2]

1. **bent :** not straight.
2. **twisted :** not the right shape.

'Very well,' Mr Utterson said. 'I have my doubts, but we'll go to the laboratory. We have to find out the truth of this matter. We'll break down the door of the laboratory, if we have to.'

'There is an axe in one of the back rooms,' said Poole. 'And we can take the metal poker from near the fire.'

Utterson nodded. He looked serious.

'This might be dangerous,' he said. 'Poole, we must be honest with each other. You haven't told me everything. The man you saw outside the laboratory – do you know who it is?'

'He moved so quickly,' began Poole. 'But, I believe it was Mr Hyde, sir. I didn't see him well. But, I think it was him. He is the only person who has the key to the laboratory. And there's something else I can't explain. A feeling. Do you know what I mean? There's something about him. It makes me feel cold.'

'I believe you,' Mr Utterson said. 'I think it was Mr Hyde, too. I fear that poor Henry Jekyll is dead. But I don't understand why Hyde is staying in the laboratory. I don't understand that at all.'

They took the axe and the poker and they went towards the back of the house. A cold wind blew along the corridors. The night was silent, but when the two men reached the laboratory door, they could hear someone walking up and down the room. Mr Utterson called out to the person behind the door.

'Jekyll! This is Utterson. Open the door. I must see you.'

A voice from behind the door answered the lawyer's command. 'No, Utterson, no!'

'That's not the voice of Henry Jekyll,' the lawyer said to Poole. 'Let's break down the door!'

Poole hit the door of the laboratory with the axe. They heard a frightened cry from the other side. The door was strong, and Poole hit it five times before it opened with a loud bang. Inside the room everything was still. They heard only the soft whistle[3] of a kettle. They saw the empty apparatus for his experiments. On the table there were some powders. The desk drawers were open.

Slowly, they moved closer to the desk, and there, in the middle of the floor, lay a man's body. It was Edward Hyde. He was dressed in the doctor's clothes. In his hand, there was a broken test tube.

'We have come too late,' Mr Utterson said to Poole. 'Hyde is dead. We must now look for the body of Dr Jekyll.'

The two men looked everywhere in the laboratory for the doctor, but they found nothing.

'Perhaps Jekyll ran away,' Mr Utterson said at last. He went to the door that opened onto the street. The door was locked, and the key was on the floor. It was impossible for someone to have left the laboratory. They returned to the laboratory and searched carefully.

'This is the medicine that Dr Jekyll ordered from the chemist,' said Poole, 'and here are the doctor's papers.'

Mr Utterson took his friend's papers and began to read them. One of them was a new will. It was similar to the will in Mr Utterson's safe. It had the same words: *In case of the death or disappearance of Henry Jekyll.* But instead of the name Edward Hyde, there was a new name in its place. The new will gave all the doctor's money to Mr John Utterson. Utterson looked at Poole and then at the paper in his hand. He could not believe it.

'I don't understand!' Mr Utterson said to Poole. 'Hyde has been here in the laboratory for a week. Why didn't he destroy this new will?'

The lawyer picked up another paper. 'This is a letter from Dr Jekyll!' he shouted to Poole. 'And look at the date on it – he wrote it today! He must still be alive!'

'It is addressed to you, sir. You should open it,' said Poole.

3. whistle : the sound of air passing through a small hole.

'I am afraid of what it might say,' said Mr Utterson quietly. 'If he has run away, then where can he hide? And what if this letter tells us something worse?' Utterson sighed heavily and opened the letter. He read the letter aloud.

My dear Utterson,

I will not be here when you read this letter. I do not know how things will end, but I know the end is near.

Lanyon told me about the letter he sent you. I want you to read it. If you wish to know more, then I leave you my confession.

Your unhappy friend,

Henry Jekyll

'Was there anything else?' Utterson asked Poole.

'There is another paper here,' Poole replied. He passed a large document to the lawyer.

'Do not talk about these papers to anyone,' Mr Utterson told the servant. 'I'll read them and then I'll decide what to do. I'll return here before midnight. Then we'll call the police.'

THINK!

Add letters to (1-6) to complete words that describe values. Then choose three of these words to complete the sentences about Poole.

1 r _ sp _ cta _ ili _ y
2 ho _ e _ ty
3 l _ y _ l _ y
4 a _ biti _ n
5 det _ rmi _ a _ i _ n
6 b _ a _ ery

In this chapter, Poole showed his (**1**) .... to find out the truth. He acted with (**2**) .... because he knew entering the laboratory could be dangerous. He also showed his (**3**) .... to his master.

Did Mr Utterson call the police when he thought Mr Hyde was in the laboratory? When he found the body? Is Mr Utterson a responsible person?

The text and beyond • page 78
Values & Feelings • page 94

CHAPTER 7

Dr Lanyon's letter

Mr Utterson locked the door of the laboratory behind him. Then he hurried[1] home and took out an envelope from his safe. He read the words on the front.

track 08

Open after the death or disappearance of Dr Henry Jekyll

Well, he didn't know for certain that Henry Jekyll was dead, but the doctor had definitely disappeared. He opened the envelope and found that there were two letters. The first was written by Dr Lanyon. It began:

1. **hurried :** went more quickly than usual.

Four days ago, on the ninth of January, I received a strange letter from Dr Jekyll. You should read this letter if you want to understand what happened afterwards.

Utterson took the second letter from the envelope. It was certainly Jekyll's writing. It had his signature. Lanyon was right that it was strange. It also looked like he had written it in a hurry. It said:

Dear Lanyon,

You are one of my oldest friends. We have quarrelled, but I still see you as a friend. I am writing now to ask you to do something for me. It is very important.

I want you to go to my house tonight. My servant Poole will be there. He knows you're coming. You and Poole must break down the door of my laboratory. Go into the laboratory alone, and from the fourth drawer of the cabinet take the powders and a book that you will see there. When you have the powders and the book, go home immediately.

At midnight, a man will come to your house. Please give him the things from my laboratory. This is all I ask you to do. If you want an explanation, the man will give you one.

Please do what I ask, Lanyon. It will save your old friend,

Henry Jekyll

Dr Lanyon's letter continued.

I thought Dr Jekyll was mad, but I decided that I ought to do what he asked, all the same.

I went to the doctor's house that night, and Poole and I went to the laboratory. We broke down the door, and I entered. I found the cabinet and took out the drawer with the powders and the book. I took it home with me.

While I waited for the man to come at midnight, I looked at the book. It seemed to be a record of the doctor's experiments. I did not understand what the doctor's experiments meant.

At midnight, there was a knock at the door of my house. I went to the door and opened it. There was a small man standing outside.

'Are you Dr Jekyll's friend?' I asked him. He moved his head. I asked him into the house. He was an ugly little man, and I did not like him. I remember that his clothes were too big for him. The man was very impatient.

'Where are the powders?' he asked me. 'Have you got them?'

'Be patient,' I told him. 'Sit down for a moment.'

'I am sorry,' the man said. 'Dr Jekyll sent me here. The business is urgent.'

I gave the powders to the man. He mixed them together in a glass, and they changed colour. The man then looked at me.

'You now have a choice,' he told me. 'I can leave the house now, and you will never know what this business is about. Or I can stay, and you will know everything. If I stay, you will

see something new to science. But I should warn you[2] – it is dreadful.'

'I'll stay,' I replied. 'I have not done all this for nothing. I want to see the end of this mystery.'

'Very well,' the man said. 'But remember, Lanyon. What you see now is a secret.'

He then drank the contents of the glass. He cried out, and almost fell to the floor. Then his body began to grow and change. The next moment I covered my face in horror.

'No!' I cried out. 'No!'

The small man who drank the powders had disappeared. There, in front of me, stood Dr Jekyll!

He told me the whole dreadful story, and even now it frightens me. What he told me made me ill. I have not slept since he told me. His story was wicked – I will not tell it to you, Utterson. I will just tell you one thing that I learnt from Dr Jekyll: the small man who came to my house that night was Edward Hyde, the murderer.

Hastie Lanyon

2. warn you : tell you that something bad might happen next.

THINK!

Tick the sentence (1-2) that best describes how Dr Lanyon feels in the sentence below.

'Then his body began to grow and change. The next moment I covered my face in horror.'

1 ☐ He is excited by the changes he has seen. He wants to know more.
2 ☐ He does not want to believe what he sees, but he knows he must.

The text and beyond • page 80
Values & Feelings • page 94

CHAPTER 8

The confession of Dr Jekyll

Mr Utterson did not doubt Dr Lanyon's story, but was this monster really Henry Jekyll? He needed to understand the story from the beginning. Slowly, he opened the papers that were with the letter and the will in the laboratory. It was Henry Jekyll's confession. He began to read.

track 09

I, Henry Jekyll, was born in 18–. I had money, I was intelligent, and I liked to work. My future seemed happy and rich.

When I was young, I wanted to be respected by my friends. I pretended to be a very serious man. I was not like other young men, who drink together and enjoy themselves. I enjoyed myself, but I kept my pleasures a secret from others. In public, I was a good man – privately, I was a bad one.

I studied science, and I became certain that all human beings are like me. Everyone has two parts – a good part, and an evil part.

No one can be happy because these two parts of nature fight against each other. In my studies I tried to separate these two parts. I wanted to create two identities. One identity would be for the good part of myself. The other identity would be for the evil part. I thought each identity would be happy: the good part would be completely good, and the evil part would be completely evil.

I worked for many years to find out how to create these new identities. I bought some special powders from a chemist in the city. Then, one night I mixed the powders together. I drank the mixture, and immediately I felt ill. Suddenly, I was a different man. I looked at myself in the mirror. I was younger and smaller, and I was completely wicked. Nothing was important to me, except pleasure. I had become Edward

Hyde! I drank another glass of the mixture, and Edward Hyde disappeared – instantly I became Dr Jekyll again.

I could now change whenever I wanted. The well-known and respected Dr Jekyll could become Edward Hyde. Edward Hyde could do things that the good doctor was not allowed to do. I began to like the new identity I had created for myself.

At first, Edward Hyde was happy just to enjoy himself, but soon he began to do terrible things. Dr Jekyll was often terrified by the things that Hyde did. The doctor could do nothing. Jekyll and Hyde were different people.

Soon I realised that Edward Hyde was dangerous. He might do something that would damage[1] the doctor's reputation. I remember the night when Hyde walked over the body of the little girl. When he had to find money to pay the girl's family, he came to the house. I decided to give Hyde a separate bank account, and to give him his own house in a different area of the city. I prepared the will which you disliked so much, Utterson. I thought I was safe.

About two months before the murder of Sir Danvers Carew, a strange thing happened. I took the powders as usual and became Edward Hyde. I went out into the city and returned home to sleep. When I woke up, I knew something was wrong. Then I looked at my hands. Dr Jekyll's hands are large, but the hands I saw were small. Then I understood: they were Edward Hyde's hands! I had gone to bed as Henry Jekyll and had woken up as Hyde! I ran to the

1. **damage :** have a bad effect on.

laboratory and took some more of the mixture. In a few minutes I was Dr Jekyll again.

Soon I understood that Hyde was stronger than Dr Jekyll. It became difficult to change back from Hyde to Dr Jekyll. Sometimes the powders did not work. I knew that I must choose between the two identities. I decided to be Dr Jekyll. For two months I followed my choice. I worked, I saw my friends, and I began to be happy again. But every day I thought about Hyde. I missed his life of pleasures – I missed the excitement of being Hyde.

One day I drank the powders again. This time, when Hyde came, he was angry. That was the night that he murdered Sir Danvers Carew. Hyde enjoyed the violence of the murder, but he was afraid of the police. He came back to the laboratory and drank the powders.

I, Henry Jekyll, remembered what Hyde had done. I was terrified. I swore [2] that I would never take the powders again. Edward Hyde was finished forever!

For a while I lived as Dr Jekyll. I worked, I saw my friends, I thought I was safe from Hyde. One day I went to the park. I sat there, thinking about my life.

'I am a good man,' I told myself. I looked at the people around me. 'I am a better man than most of them,' I thought. At that instant, I suddenly felt ill. Then I felt a change in myself. I looked down – I had become Hyde once more!

I was Edward Hyde, and the police in London were looking everywhere for me! London was dangerous for Edward Hyde the murderer. I needed the powders from the laboratory. But how was I going to get them? I did not trust the servants.

Then I had an idea. I remembered Dr Lanyon. He could go to

2. swore : promised (see *swear*, p.44).

the laboratory for me! I went to a hotel, and I wrote a letter to Dr Lanyon. I asked him to go to the laboratory, and to bring the powders to his house. The doctor did what I asked.

As soon as I took the powders in the doctor's house, I was Dr Jekyll once more. When Dr Lanyon saw what happened when I took the powders, he was shocked. My old friend was frightened of me.

I went back to the laboratory. Now a terrible time began for me. Hyde was strong now, and he often came back. If I slept, I woke up to discover that I was Hyde. At the same time, Dr Jekyll became ill and weak. Sometimes the powders did not work.

Hyde and I lived together in the laboratory. We hated each other, and we feared each other. I feared him because he was evil. He feared me because I wanted to be good. Hyde wanted to live, and he was afraid of the police. I wanted to die, and Hyde was afraid that I would kill myself. He needed my body to live.

Then I used the last of the powders. I sent Poole to the chemist to buy more. The new powders did not work. I sent him to another chemist, but they still did not work. Again and again I sent Poole to look for the powders, but the result was always the same. Perhaps the original powders contained an impurity – and it was the impurity that made them work.

I know the end is close. I will soon become Edward Hyde again. Without the powders, I will be Edward Hyde forever. He will sit here in my laboratory, and he will be afraid of the police. He, too, knows that the end is close. If the police find him, he will die in prison. Or maybe he will kill himself. I, Henry Jekyll, do not know. It is not important to me. These are the last moments of the life of your old friend.

Now I will put down my pen and put an end to the unhappy life of Henry Jekyll.

THINK!

Unscramble the letters to make words about good and evil. (The first letter is done for you.) Is it possible to be both good and evil?

1 vileenoc **2** kidsenns **3** hrorro **4** cuyerlt **5** loev **6** rcepest

Do you agree/disagree with this sentence? Explain your answers.

'If you stop a person from doing something, they will only want to do it more.'

The text and beyond • page 82
Values & Feelings • page 94

Old Town, Edinburgh

Deacon Brodie

Robert Louis Stevenson grew up in the New Town of the City of Edinburgh. Although the New Town was wealthier than the poorer, dirtier, narrow streets of the Old Town, the two parts of the city were connected. People from the Old Town worked in the large houses of the New Town. Stevenson spent time in the Old Town when he was a student. He saw for himself the respectable people who went there because it was exciting or different from the New Town. Stevenson was interested in the tales of the 'darker' side of the city's history. One of these stories was the double life of Deacon Brodie.

Deacon Brodie

William Brodie lived in Edinburgh from 1741 to 1788. He made beautiful furniture for wealthy families in Edinburgh. He was an important member of a trade guild[1] (a Deacon) and a member of the city council.[2] However, there was a secret side to Brodie's life. He was also a gambler[3] who lived an extravagant lifestyle.[4] As well as furniture, he made and repaired locks. He started to copy the keys to people's houses and shops that he worked for. He was a respectable gentleman by day and a burglar by night.

Brodie worked with other criminals. He organised their activities and gave them the information they needed. One night, Brodie and his assistants took some pistols and tried to steal money from Edinburgh's Excise Office.[5] The robbery did not happen as Brodie had hoped and two of his assistants were caught. They told the police everything. Brodie escaped to the Netherlands where he

1. **trade guild :** an official organisation for people with the same job. (These used to be powerful in cities.)
2. **council :** a group of people who control a city or a town.
3. **gambler :** someone who wins or loses money on the result of games, e.g. cards.
4. **extravagant lifestyle :** spending more money than he needed to, e.g. on luxuries.
5. **Excise Office :** a place where money from taxes is kept.

▸ Old Town, Edinburgh

was arrested and returned to Edinburgh. The punishment for his crimes at that time was death (execution). But Brodie thought he could escape death. He wore a metal ring around his neck before his execution. He paid the executioner to continue even though he knew about the ring. His body was removed quickly by the executioner, but it was too late. The metal ring did not save him and he died.

Like everyone in Edinburgh, Stevenson knew the story about Deacon Brodie. He probably heard it many times when he was a child. But Stevenson also had a personal interest in Brodie. Brodie had made some furniture for Stevenson's father and this furniture was still in the family home when he was a boy. Stevenson even wrote a short play about Brodie's life when he was younger. In fact, some people believe that Stevenson used the idea of Brodie's double life when he wrote *The Strange Case of Dr Jekyll and Mr Hyde*.

1 Answer the following questions.

1. Where did Stevenson grow up?
2. Was Brodie a respectable member of society? Give examples.
3. How was Brodie able to steal from people's houses?
4. How did Brodie try to escape death?
5. What was the connection of Stevenson's father to Brodie?
6. Did Stevenson write about Brodie?

2 Discuss the questions.

1. In Edinburgh there is an Old Town and a New Town. How is this similar to the description of the different streets in London in *The Strange Case of Dr Jekyll and Mr Hyde*?
2. Can you think of an example of people who seem to be good, but have done bad things in: a) fiction; b) the news?

Mad scientists and monsters: 'Frankenstein'

Frankenstein's 'creature'

At the time Stevenson wrote *The Strange Case of Dr Jekyll and Mr Hyde*, many people believed that it was dangerous for scientists to try to understand things that were outside of human control. This is also true today. In books and films, it is not unusual to find the character of the 'mad scientist'. The scientists in these stories usually have good intentions. But although they try to push the limits of science and find new ways of doing things, sometimes their actions can be dangerous, and they might even find out it is too late to change what they have done.

In Mary Shelley's novel *Frankenstein* (1818), the scientist Victor Frankenstein tells how he went beyond[1] limits in science that 'ought not to be crossed'. The story begins with the letters of Captain Robert Walton. His ship is in the Arctic and he can't move because of the ice, so he writes to his sister. In his letters, he tells her about a surprise meeting with a man called Victor Frankenstein. Walton tells his story.

Victor Frankenstein is a clever young scientist, but soon he becomes interested in darker things. He makes a human body from dead bodies and he brings it to life.[2] Victor runs away and 'the creature' leaves Victor's apartment. Later, Victor's brother is murdered by the creature. The creature asks Victor to make a female companion. Victor wants to do this, but then he changes his ideas about this plan. The creature is angry and he kills Victor's fiancée the night before the

1. beyond : past/further than a point.
2. brings it to life : makes it come alive.

scientist is going to get married. Victor tries to find the creature to get his revenge.[3] He dies shortly after he has told his story to Walton. In the novel, the creature also tells his story. When his creator dies, he is sad that he is dead and he feels alone.

Mary Shelley's tale of the scientist and the monster he creates is one of the earliest examples of a type of writing which was later called 'science fiction'. In *Frankenstein*, the results of going beyond these 'limits' in science is used as a warning[4] to others. In other words, it is dangerous to experiment with things we don't understand because there could be terrible consequences.[5] Perhaps, though, the story asks more important questions about the responsibility of human beings for their own creations.

---

3. revenge : an action to punish him because he did bad things.
4. warning : something that tells of the bad things that might happen.
5. consequences : results.

1 Comprehension • Read the sentences. Decide if they are true (T) or false (F). If the answer is not in the text, choose doesn't say (D).

	T	F	D
1. In the 19th century, scientific discoveries were mostly a good thing for the rich.	☐	☐	☐
2. The first part of the story of *Frankenstein* is told by Robert Walton's sister.	☐	☐	☐
3. The monster in Mary Shelley's novel is called Victor.	☐	☐	☐
4. The monster also tells his story.	☐	☐	☐
5. *Frankenstein* is an early example of 'science fiction' writing.	☐	☐	☐
6. Science fiction was a popular form of writing in the 19th century.	☐	☐	☐

2 Film project • There are many different film versions of *Frankenstein*. Find one of them to watch. Write a film review. What do you like/dislike about it? Does the director try and make the film more modern? Is it similar to the description of the book or does it include new and different scenes?

Activities

68 **The text and beyond**

Chapter 1 68
Chapter 2 70
Chapter 3 72
Chapter 4 74
Chapter 5 76
Chapter 6 78
Chapter 7 80
Chapter 8 82

84 **Extensive listening**

86 **Surf the net**

87 **Trinity** • Preparation

88 **Preliminary** • Preparation

91 **Exit test** • Let's revise the story

94 **Values & Feelings**

Chapter 1

THE TEXT AND BEYOND

1 Comprehension Check • Read the sentences. Decide if they are true (T) or false (F). Correct the false ones.

	T	F
1. Mr Utterson and Mr Enfield meet for their usual Sunday afternoon walk.	☐	☐
2. The house they stopped at was a different colour to the other houses.	☐	☐
3. The old man was angry with the little girl because she did not look where she was going.	☐	☐
4. The crowd asked the man to look after the little girl.	☐	☐
5. The cheque the man wrote was a forgery.	☐	☐
6. Mr Utterson didn't ask who wrote the cheque because he already knew who it was.	☐	☐

2 Viewpoints • Read the stories from different people who saw the little girl being hurt. Some of the details are different to Mr Enfield's story. Underline the parts that are different as in the example.

0. 'It was terrible. A <u>really big, wide</u> man came down the street and he <u>hit my sister in the face</u>. She fell to the ground, but he didn't stop.'
   a really small, ugly man/walked over my sister
1. 'I was talking to a neighbour and this man came around the corner – he looked like a horrible man – and he didn't look where he was going. He crashed into a little girl and then he stood on her and broke her leg.'
2. 'We were all angry with him. He didn't say sorry. We said we were going to tell the police, but he asked us not to say anything.'
3. 'I saw two men come out of the house with him. Then the man gave the child's father a cheque for one hundred pounds.'

3 Writing • Imagine you were there. Write your own story about the events that Mr Enfield tells. You can add some new facts of your own.

4 Vocabulary • Use the puzzle to help you find opposites of the words in the box. What name does the puzzle spell in blue?

honest bright pretty generous rude clean

1								A			
2					I						
3			D		S						
4				G							
5							A	R	K		
6	P					E					

5 Adjectives • Use the adjectives from exercise 4 to describe characters and/or places in Chapter 1.

e.g. Mr Utterson was honest. The street was pretty.

6 Speaking • Describe the houses. Find different ways of comparing them.

e.g. ... is taller than ...
It is more/less/not as ...
I'd rather live in ... than ...

Chapter 2

THE TEXT AND BEYOND

1 Comprehension Check • Choose the correct word in italics to make logical questions about Chapter 2.

1. *Why / When* was Mr Utterson unhappy about the will?
   His client Dr Jekyll had left ....
2. *Where / What* else worried Mr Utterson about the will?
   If Mr Jekyll disappeared, ...
3. *Who / Why* did Mr Utterson go to see next?
   His friend ....
4. *When / Why* didn't Dr Lanyon and Dr Jekyll see each other often?
   Dr Lanyon didn't like ....
5. *Where / Why* did Mr Utterson meet Mr Hyde?
   He met him in the ....
6. *Which / Where* part of the house did Mr Hyde have a key to?
   He had a key to ....
7. *How / When* did Dr Jekyll speak to Mr Utterson?
   He spoke to him after ....
8. *Why / What* did Dr Jekyll ask the lawyer to do?
   He asked him to promise ....

2 Vocabulary • Find the meaning of any new words in the box. Then complete the sentences with the best word.

witness death client executor signature inheritance possessions

1. The news of the .... of the famous scientist appeared in all the newspapers.
2. A rich banker left his .... to his four sons. They each received one million pounds.
3. To complete a will, you need the .... of a ....
4. In a will you can give instructions about your money and ....
5. The .... of the wealthy businessman was surprised to hear he had died.
6. The person who follows the instructions in a will is called an ....

3 Gap fill • Complete the will using words from the clues and information from the text in Chapter 2. Do not use a word more than once.

In the event of my **(1)** d.................., my **(2)** i.................. will go to my **(3)** f.................., **(4)** Mr E.................. **(5)** H.................. . Or, if I **(6)** d.................. for more than three months, then Mr Edward Hyde will inherit all my **(7)** m.................. and my **(8)** p.................. .

I have signed this will in front of my lawyer and **(9)** w.................., Mr John Utterson. Mr Utterson has agreed to follow these instructions as the **(10)** e.................. of this will.

4 Characters • In Chapter 2, Mr Utterson tries to find answers to the mystery of the will. Who does he speak to? Write your answers in the gaps (1-4). Then match the quotes (a-d) to the person who says them.

1. ☐ ....

2. ☐ ....

3. ☐ ....

4. ☐ ....

a 'You do not understand my position.'

b 'Dr Jekyll is not at home.'

c 'He has such strange ideas.'

d 'Mr Hyde never dines here.'

5 Detective work • Imagine you are a private investigator. You have been asked to find information about Mr Hyde. Write some questions to ask the people Mr Utterson speaks to. Who else could you ask to find out more about Mr Hyde and his life?

6 Speaking • Dr Jekyll and Dr Lanyon are both scientists, but they don't always agree with each other. Read the statements about science. Do you agree with them? Why?/Why not? Discuss with another student.

1. Life is better today than in the past because we understand more about science.
2. Science can answer questions we haven't asked yet.
3. Scientists do experiments for good reasons. It is other people who do bad things with their discoveries.

Chapter 3

THE TEXT AND BEYOND

1 Comprehension Check • Are the following sentences true (T) or false (F)? Correct the false ones.

	T	F
1. The girl saw the attack from her bedroom window.	☐	☐
2. The maid recognised Mr Hyde because he knew her employer.	☐	☐
3. The old man attacked Mr Hyde first.	☐	☐
4. The police thought Mr Utterson was the murderer.	☐	☐
5. Mr Utterson knew Sir Danvers Carew because he was his client.	☐	☐
6. Mr Hyde had no money and nowhere to go.	☐	☐
7. Dr Jekyll wanted to find Mr Hyde.	☐	☐
8. Mr Utterson asked the servant if someone had arrived with a letter.	☐	☐

2 Gap fill • Complete the sentences with words from Chapter 3.

1. '.............................. because he sometimes came to the house where she ...., to speak to her ....'
2. 'The .... had gone, but the old .... was .... in the street.'
3. 'When the .... know of this, everyone will be talking about it.'
4. 'I .... the envelope,' Dr .... told him, 'but the letter was not ....'
5. 'Someone .... a letter. What did the man .... ?'

3 Interpretation • Answer the questions about sentences (1-5) in exercise 2.

1. The maid's employer knew Mr Hyde. Do you think her employer was also a bad man?
2. Does the reader know that Sir Danvers Carew was murdered before we read this sentence?
3. Why is the policeman worried?
4. Do you believe Dr Jekyll's story?
5. Why did Mr Utterson ask the servant this question?

4 Reading • Read about the people (1-3). Find a tour (a-d) for them that matches their interests and their availability. There is one you will not need.

1. ☐ Sohil likes reading Victorian detective stories. He is looking for a fun tour that includes the places he reads about in fiction. He is free at weekends and would like to go in a group. He is a student and doesn't have much money.
2. ☐ Marzia wants a private guided tour so that she can do her own private investigations! She would like to visit some of the locations of stories about murders and mysteries in London. She only has one free afternoon before she returns to Milan.
3. ☐ Kevin is writing a book about crime in Victorian London. He would like to know about other unusual mysteries and crimes in the east of the city. He likes going to museums and galleries and he often goes to the library. He is free on Sundays.

a Victorian Crime in East London: Exhibition and Tour

The ticket for the Victorian Crime exhibition includes hourly tours of the area in the east of London near the museum showing the exhibition on a weekend. The tour guides are friendly and know a lot about the subject. The shop has books and souvenirs from the exhibition.

b Sherlock Uncovered

This is a walking tour of the places in a recent television series about the fictional detective, Sherlock Holmes. The tour takes place every Saturday at 11 am. It is free, but it is very popular, so it is best to book in advance.

c Independent Mystery Tours

These are private tours by taxi. You can book any time for as long as you want, from one hour to a full day. The drivers are very knowledgeable. They will take you to any locations you ask to see. They will take you to ones you don't know, too!

d Crime Tour: Victorian London

This full-day bus tour runs every Thursday and costs £25. The tour takes people to fictional and real places in stories about crime in Victorian London. It includes places in the stories of Charles Dickens, the real lives of criminals in the books about Sherlock Holmes and a visit to East London to find out the secrets of Jack the Ripper.

Chapter 4 THE TEXT AND BEYOND

1 Comprehension Check • Reorder these words to make questions about Chapter 4. Answer the questions.

1. the/Mr Hyde/from/letter/wrote/Who?
2. the/Did/Mr Hyde/find/police?
3. of/eighth/What/January/the/happened/on?
4. did/Dr Lanyon/was/say/Why/going to/he/die?
5. What/did/from/do/with/Mr Utterson/letter/Dr Lanyon/the?
6. time/did/spend/Dr Jekyll/Where/his?

2 Summary • The pictures (a-f) relate to events in Chapter 4. Number them in the order the events happen in the story.

a

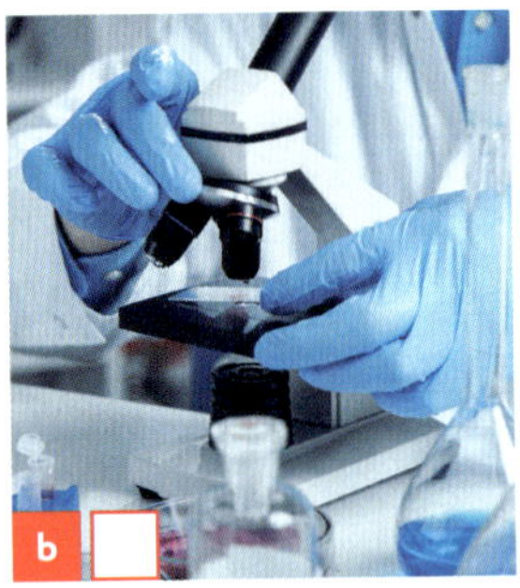
b

c

d

e

f

3 Writing • Write a sentence for each of the events above as in the example.

e.g. Dr Jekyll invited his friends to dinner.

Should and *ought to*

'I don't think we ***should*** talk about this to anyone.'

If you tell someone he/she *should* (or *shouldn't*) do something, you are saying it is (or isn't) a good thing to do. We can also use *ought to*. *Should* and *ought to* are modal verbs. We can use them:

- to make a **suggestion**: *You **should** try the cake! It's nice.*
- to provide **advice**: *You **ought to** see your doctor.*
- for **moral obligation**: *You **shouldn't** lie.*

4 Grammar • Match sentences (1-4) with (a-d).

1. ☐ You shouldn't break the rules.
2. ☐ You should buy that coat.
3. ☐ You shouldn't have told her.
4. ☐ You ought to say sorry to her.

a Maybe she will understand.
b They are made for a reason.
c It looks good on you.
d It was a secret.

5 Vocabulary and speaking • Add words under the two headings. Then work with a partner. He/She wants to be healthier. Offer some advice.

Healthy mind	Healthy body
feel *happy/less stressed*	eat ....
talk to	go to ....
stop	visit the ....
....	....

Chapter 5

THE TEXT AND BEYOND

1 Comprehension Check • Choose the correct word in italics so the questions about Chapter 5 make logical sense. Then answer the questions.

1. What did Mr Enfield find out about the *laboratory / experiments*?
2. Where did the two friends go after Mr Enfield told his story about the *garden / door*?
3. What happened when Mr Utterson and Mr Enfield *saw / heard* Dr Jekyll?
4. Why did the *maid / servant* come to the lawyer's house?
5. What does Poole say about the *sound / voice* in the laboratory?
6. What did the doctor ask his servant to get from the *chemist / house*?
7. What did the *envelope / note* say?
8. Does Poole think the *handwriting / sample* is important?

2 Reading pictures • Look at the pictures on pages 38 and 39. Answer the questions.

1. Why is the maid upset?
2. Who is at the window? What is happening?

3 Titles • Read the title for Chapter 5 and answer the questions.

1. Describe the location of the laboratory.
2. Who uses the laboratory?
3. Who do you think is the man in the laboratory at the end of Chapter 5?

4 Characters • Who do the sentences describe? What is the character's motivation (the reason they act, think or feel this way)?

1. He said that he would rather not see Mr Hyde again.
2. He said that he knows the door is at the back of Dr Jekyll's house.
3. He refused to come down to speak to Mr Utterson and Mr Enfield.
4. He came to Mr Utterson's house.
5. He asked his servant to bring notes to the chemist's.

5 Adverbs • Underline the adverbs you find in the sentences. Which of the sentences do not contain adverbs?

1. Dr Jekyll closed the window with a bang.
2. Mr Enfield nodded seriously.
3. Mr Utterson was sitting quietly by the fire.
4. Explain everything to me. And try to stay calm.
5. When she saw Mr Utterson, one of the servant girls began to cry.
6. Poole knocked nervously on the door of the laboratory.

6 Writing • Rewrite the sentences in exercise 5 that do not contain adverbs. You can change or remove words, but you must include at least one adverb in the new sentence.

e.g. When he saw me, he ran back into the laboratory and closed the door.
→ When he saw me, he ran ***quickly*** *back to the laboratory and closed the door* ***firmly****.*

7 Weather • Weather is important in the story. It creates suspense. (Suspense gives us a feeling of anxiety or excitement about what might happen.) Describe the weather on the night Mr Utterson goes with Poole to Dr Jekyll's house. Is the weather in the story mostly bad weather or good weather?

8 Vocabulary • Complete the sentences (1-6) with a weather word. Underline any new words. Use a dictionary if necessary.

1. The mist and .... fell across the city like a blanket.
2. The .... blew hard. Suddenly, a strong breeze pushed the door shut with a bang.
3. A snowstorm brought hail and sleet from the east. The tall roofs were covered in ....
4. The road was frozen and it was difficult to walk on the hard ....
5. High pressure brought hot weather, but she knew that soon a .... was coming.
6. The thunder roared and .... lit up the sky.

Chapter 6

THE TEXT AND BEYOND

1 Comprehension Check • Match the beginning of each sentence (1-6) to (a-f). Then complete the sentences using your own words.

1. ☐ Utterson thought that maybe the illness
2. ☐ Poole was certain that the man
3. ☐ The lawyer and the servant decided to
4. ☐ When they moved closer to the desk,
5. ☐ They found a new will
6. ☐ Mr Utterson told Poole not to speak to

a they saw, in the middle of the room, ...

b in the laboratory was not his ....

c leaving Dr Jekyll's money to ....

d anyone; he would call the police when ....

e break down the door with ....

f had changed the doctor's ....

2 Reading • Read part of Mr Utterson's diary. Then answer the questions (1-4).

A very strange night indeed! There are still so many unanswered questions. My poor friend, Henry Jekyll, has disappeared. But the door was locked and the key was on the floor, so how did he escape? Did Mr Hyde die drinking the mixture of the powders? He must have taken them just before we entered. But was it his voice we heard, and why didn't he destroy the will? What if people think I am the murderer? I must solve this mystery!

1. Do you think Mr Utterson's diary is like the notes of a detective, a lawyer or a friend?
2. Mr Utterson asks a lot of questions. If he finds the answer to these questions, do you think he will solve the mystery?
3. Is there a question he hasn't asked?
4. Do you have any suggestions to his questions?

Past perfect simple

'... the doctor ***had*** definitely ***disappeared***.'

When we are telling a story in the past, we use the **past perfect simple** (*had* + past participle) to describe an event or action that happened earlier than another past event or past action.

*We saw that he **had left** some powders on the desk. (He left the powders on the desk before we came to the room and saw them.)*

3 Grammar • Use the pictures to help you complete the sentences (1-6) using a verb in the past perfect simple and other words.

1. I .... (*buy*) .... two days before I became ill. We all had colds that year.
2. We tried to get in, but he .... (*lock*) ....
3. He was so angry. He couldn't believe someone .... (*break*) ....
4. He didn't know about the inheritance. She .... (*change*) her ....
5. He was lucky to find very loyal staff. They .... (*work*) in the .... for years.
6. When the .... arrived, the thief .... (*disappear*).

Chapter 7

THE TEXT AND BEYOND

1 Comprehension Check • Read the sentences and answer true (T) or false (F). Correct the false sentences.

	T	F
1. Mr Utterson only reads one of the two letters in the envelope.	☐	☐
2. The letter from Dr Jekyll asks Dr Lanyon to help him because he is a friend.	☐	☐
3. The servant comes into the room with Mr Utterson when he gets the powders.	☐	☐
4. The man who comes to Dr Lanyon's house was wearing clothes that were old.	☐	☐
5. The man is impatient because he needs the powders.	☐	☐
6. Dr Lanyon wants to know more about the reason the man had come.	☐	☐
7. Dr Lanyon sees Dr Jekyll become Mr Hyde.	☐	☐
8. Dr Lanyon doesn't know that the man is Mr Hyde.	☐	☐

2 Characters • Who is this? Write *L* for Dr Lanyon, *H* for Mr Hyde or *J* for Dr Jekyll.

1. ☐ He asked another scientist to help him.
2. ☐ He broke down the door of the laboratory.
3. ☐ He asked him to give him the powders.
4. ☐ He said that he would show him something new to science.
5. ☐ He became the doctor once again.
6. ☐ He was shocked by what he saw.

3 Role play • Imagine the scene from the point where the man arrives at Dr Lanyon's house to the end of Chapter 7. With another student, write some lines of conversation between the two men. Act out the scene.

4 Vocabulary • Find the words in the box in a dictionary. Then complete the text with a word from the box.

body physicist horror shape radiation wolf viewers superheroes transformation villains comics destroy

In *The Strange Case of Dr Jekyll and Mr Hyde*, we hear from Dr Lanyon about the night he meets Mr Hyde and his frightening **(1)** .... into Dr Henry Jekyll. Ever since Stevenson's story was published, this tale of transformation has fascinated **(2)** .... of film and television, as well as readers and writers of books and **(3)** .... Stories of transformation exist in ancient stories as well as new ones. Sometimes a person's **(4)** .... changes, but other times it is their personality that changes, too.

In films, we can see examples of this in **(5)** .... films and tales of **(6)** .... Werewolf stories, where a person becomes a **(7)** .... when the moon is full, often show how the transformation happens. Like with Jekyll, who changes his body **(8)** .... when he becomes Hyde, the transformation is often scary and unpleasant. In comic books, one famous superhero is a scientist who becomes a huge green monster. Dr Bruce Banner is a bright young **(9)** .... who is exposed to **(10)** .... during an experiment. Banner is weak and shy, but later he becomes the Hulk who is big and strong. He finds that he cannot control this change. If his heart beats quickly, or he is angry or sad, he transforms into this superhuman being. Although Hulk can **(11)** .... things without thinking, he can also be useful when he fights against evil **(12)** ....

5 Speaking • Answer the questions.

1. Can you think of any books or films where the character changes?
2. What changes – his/her body, his/her personality, or both these things?

6 Writing • Use your discussion to write about one of your favourite superheroes or horror films where a person transforms.

Chapter 8

THE TEXT AND BEYOND

1 Comprehension Check • Choose the best answer, a, b or c.

1. Describe Henry Jekyll when he was younger.
   - a ☐ He only liked serious people.
   - b ☐ He wasn't very well liked.
   - c ☐ He pretended to be good when he wasn't.
2. What did Dr Jekyll want to do?
   - a ☐ separate good and evil into two parts
   - b ☐ change into a good man all the time
   - c ☐ create lots of different identities
3. When did Dr Jekyll realise Hyde was dangerous?
   - a ☐ soon after he first became Hyde
   - b ☐ when he killed Sir Danvers Carew
   - c ☐ when he wrote the will and Mr Utterson was worried
4. What happened when Dr Jekyll was in the park?
   - a ☐ He decided he would never be evil again.
   - b ☐ He became so ill that he fainted.
   - c ☐ He became Mr Hyde without taking the powders.
5. What did Dr Jekyll realise later?
   - a ☐ He couldn't change back when he wanted.
   - b ☐ He had killed his friend Dr Lanyon.
   - c ☐ The powders were impure so now they didn't work.
6. What did Dr Jekyll say at the end of his confession?
   - a ☐ The powders would kill him.
   - b ☐ The police would find him in the laboratory.
   - c ☐ As Dr Jekyll his life would come to an end.

Would and *could*

'Hyde was afraid that I *would* kill myself.'

We can use the modal verbs *would* and *could* to make **hypotheses about the future**. When we make a hypothesis, we are guessing something will happen, but we can't know for certain because it hasn't happened yet.

2 Grammar • Match the sentences (1-4) and (a-d). Add *would ('d)/wouldn't* to complete the sentences.

1. ☐ I think you should study Science and Maths.
2. ☐ You like to look after people.
3. ☐ I don't think I could live in a city.
4. ☐ I'd like to be famous. I'd be the same person.

a You .... (*be*) a good doctor because you're clever and you care.
b I .... (*change*) who I am, but I .... (*have*) more money.
c Those subjects .... (*help*) you to become a scientist.
d I .... (*be*) lonely and I .... (*have*) any friends.

3 Speaking • Scientists use hypotheses to make suggestions when they can't show something is true yet. Look at these possible events in the future. If these things happened, would it be good or bad? Discuss.

1. Parts of the body could grow in a laboratory.
2. Robots could think and feel like humans.
3. We could decide which characteristics we want/don't want in our children.
4. We could change things like computer passwords using our brains.

EXTENSIVE LISTENING +

track 10

1 Listen to the conversations and put a tick in the box below the correct picture.

1. Which picture best matches the description of the house?

a

b

c

2. Who are the two people describing?

a

b

c

3. What is Sarah going to help Rahim with?

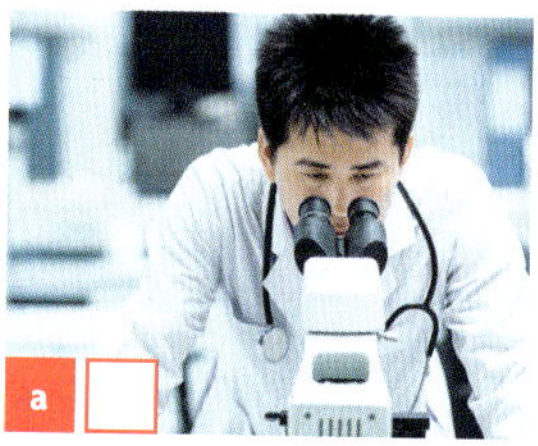
a

b

c

4. What are the two men looking for?

a

b

c

track 11

2 You will hear an online radio discussion about a murder case. Choose a person (a-d) for each statement (1-8).

a Jane **b** Paula **c** Pete **d** Bill

This person:

1. ☐ is the presenter of the show.
2. ☐ doesn't seem to trust lawyers very much.
3. ☐ thinks it is more important that the victim was the man's wife.
4. ☐ thinks it is easier to behave like a criminal if you know the law.
5. ☐ feels that the newspapers are saying something that is dangerous.
6. ☐ allows people to explain their point of view.
7. ☐ says that all suspects are investigated, sometimes even the police.
8. ☐ thinks that things like this shouldn't happen again.

track 12

3 You will hear two students, Katie and Paul, talking about *The Strange Case of Dr Jekyll and Mr Hyde*. After listening to their discussion, complete the sentences in your own words using your own opinions.

1. I think that the main themes in this discussion were ....
2. I agree with .... about ....
3. I don't agree that ....
4. I found it interesting that ....
5. If I was having this discussion, I would also say that ....

track 13

4 You will hear two friends talking about detective stories. Before you listen, answer questions (1-2). After you have listened to the conversation, answer questions (3-5).

1. What happens in detective stories?
2. What type of characters are there, e.g. a detective, etc.?
3. What do the people speaking like about detective stories?
4. Which other detective do the friends talk about?
5. Do you think *The Strange Case of Dr Jekyll and Mr Hyde* is like a detective story?

Scottish writers

Scotland has many places connected to writers and writing and a long history of famous authors.
You can find museums, statues, a Writers' Museum and even an entire town full of bookshops.
Surf the net and find out more about the places, the writers and their stories.

Work with a partner. Use an internet search engine to answer the following questions.

1. Where is the Writers' Museum? What are the opening times?
2. Who is often described as Scotland's National Poet? Where is his birthplace?
3. Where can you find Scotland's National Book Town?
4. Which character was created by J.M. Barrie? Where can you see a statue of this character?
5. Which famous Scottish writer is remembered with a tall monument in the centre of Edinburgh?
6. Which famous modern female author wrote a story about a young magician when she lived in Edinburgh? Clue: the films also show places in Scotland. Can you find any examples?
7. Can you find any other female authors or poets connected with Scotland?
8. Find out more information about Robert Louis Stevenson and his travels.

TRINITY • Preparation

1 GESE Grade 5 – Recent personal experiences • The letters of Dr Lanyon and Dr Jekyll describe their own personal experiences of an event. Use the questions to help you describe your recent personal experiences.

1. Have you ever felt scared or angry? What made you feel this way?
2. Has anything really interesting or unusual happened to you this year?

2 GESE Grade 6 – Money • Dr Jekyll uses his money to live a double life as Mr Hyde. Complete the questions about money with words from the box. Practise asking and answering the questions with another student.

monthly cash machine lend phone bought withdraw

1. Have you ever used a .... to .... money?
2. What do you buy? For example, ... , weekly, every day?
3. What things have you .... recently?
4. Do you think it's a good idea to .... someone money?
5. Do you ever pay for things with your .... ? How do you think we will pay for things in ten years' time?

3 GESE Grade 6 – Rules and regulations • In the story, Mr Hyde breaks the law. Look at the examples (a-c). What might happen if you break these rules? Then answer the questions (1-2).

a A person does not stop at a traffic light.
b A person doesn't buy a ticket on a train.
c A person sells medicine for themselves to another person.

1. Have you ever been in trouble because you didn't follow a rule? What happened?
2. What are you doing tomorrow? Do any of the places you are going to have rules?

e.g. I'm going swimming tomorrow. At the swimming pool you can't run because it's dangerous.

CHAPTERS 1-3

1 Reading Part 1 • For each question, choose the correct answer.

0. Why has Richard sent this text?

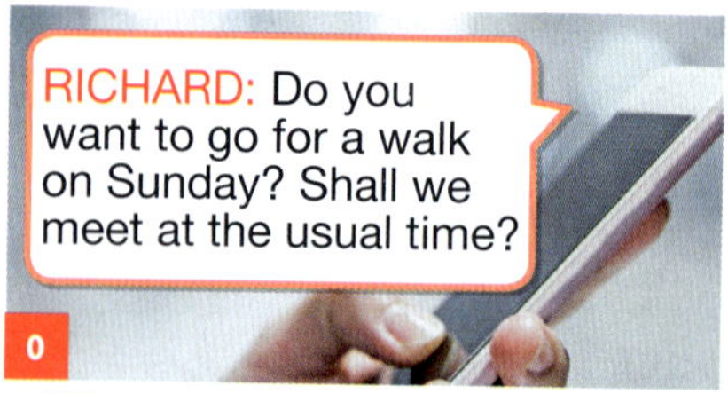

- a ✔ To invite his friend to go for a walk.
- b ☐ He is always bored on Sundays.
- c ☐ To change the time he is meeting his friend.

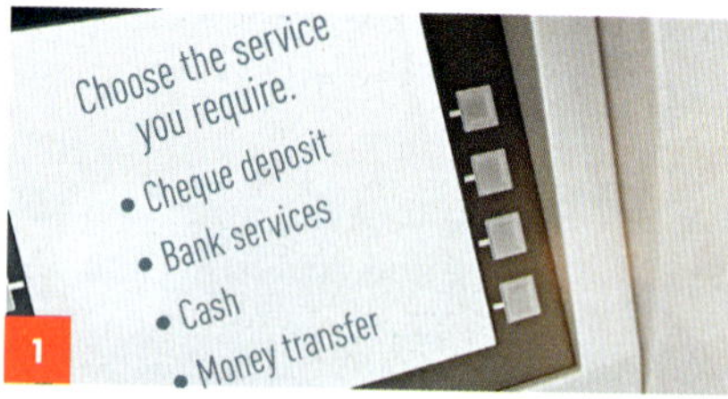

- a ☐ You can only take out money from this machine.
- b ☐ You should use this service for cheques.
- c ☐ It costs money to use this machine.

- a ☐ The payment was made last year.
- b ☐ This is the first payment.
- c ☐ All wills cost £120.

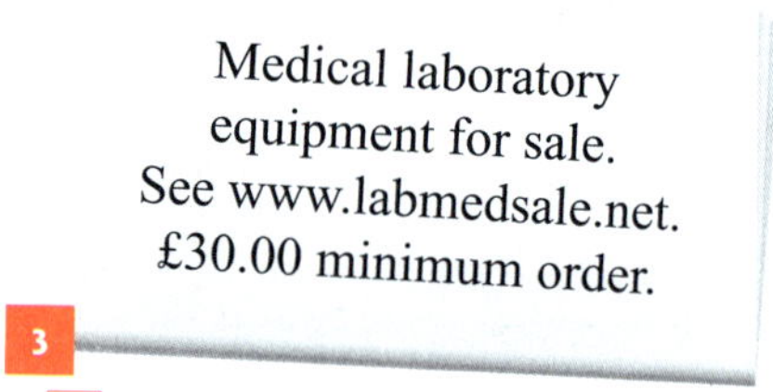

- a ☐ You can buy any type of equipment.
- b ☐ It is cheaper if you use the website.
- c ☐ You must spend £30 or more.

- a ☐ The rooms are in a nice area of town.
- b ☐ All rooms have comfortable furniture.
- c ☐ You don't have to rent a room with furniture.

- a ☐ You must use a different entrance.
- b ☐ The building is closed.
- c ☐ The building only has one entrance.

CHAPTERS 4-8

1 Reading Part 5 • For each question, choose the correct answer.

GOTHIC NOVELS

Early examples **(0)** ......*of*...... gothic literature date from the 18th century, but Gothic literature was also popular in the 19th century. Gothic novels sometimes describe frightening or horrible events. Although some of these frightening events happen in strange and mysterious **(1)** .... , others feel familiar. The dark, foggy streets of Stevenson's novel, *The Strange Case of Dr Jekyll and Mr Hyde*, **(2)** .... familiar to readers of 19th-century London. They understood the feeling of **(3)** .... scared in an empty street on a dark, windy night. A theme of many gothic novels is the existence of a secret. Often people are confused about **(4)** .... secret. They understand that something is wrong, but **(5)** .... don't believe their feelings. In *The Strange Case of Dr Jekyll and Mr Hyde* for example, Mr Utterson **(6)** .... that Dr Jekyll is hiding something from him. However, he finds it difficult to believe the truth until he reads Dr Jekyll's confession.

0.	(a) of	b on	c by	d at
1.	a house	b places	c space	d events
2.	a not	b was	c there	d were
3.	a being	b knowing	c be	d feel
4.	a these	b those	c this	d its
5.	a it	b they	c he	d them
6.	a believe	b knows	c stops	d feel

2 Writing Part 3 • Your English teacher has asked you to write a story. Your story must begin with this sentence:

There was something strange about that man.

Write your story.

3 Speaking Part 3 • A group of friends are going to do an experiment. Below are some things they might bring with them. Talk with another student about what they should take. Which of these things are safe in a laboratory?

1

2

3

4

5

6

4 Reading Part 6 • For each question, write the correct answer. Write one word for each gap.

A BOOK REVIEW: *THE ISLAND OF DR MOREAU*

One of (**0**) ......my.... favourite books is *The Island of Dr Moreau* by H.G. Wells. The story is (**1**) .... an Englishman, Edward Prendick. He is saved by another ship when he (**2**).............. lost at sea. He meets a man called Montgomery who is taking a cargo of animals to a scientist, Dr Moreau, on (**3**) .... island in the Pacific. When they arrive at the island, he finds out that (**4**) .... evil Dr Moreau is doing horrible experiments. Moreau tells Prendick that he is trying to create new creatures. He hopes that one day, they will become like human beings. Prendick tries to escape, but before he leaves the island, he meets some (**5**) .... Dr Moreau's interesting creations. It is really scary, but it is fun (**6**).............. read!

EXIT TEST

LET'S REVISE THE STORY

1 Picture summary • The following pictures are not in the right order. Put them in the order they appear in the book and write a short summary under each one to say what's happening.

2 Comprehension check • Answer the questions about the story. Number the sentences with the chapter number where you find the information to the question. You can use some chapters more than once.

1. ☐ Why did Dr Jekyll want to create two identities?
2. ☐ What did Dr Jekyll ask Poole to get?
3. ☐ What did Mr Hyde do to the girl in Mr Enfield's story?
4. ☐ When did Dr Jekyll realise he was changing into Hyde without the mixture?
5. ☐ Why was Mr Utterson worried about Dr Jekyll's will?
6. ☐ Who did Mr Hyde murder and what did the man do?
7. ☐ What did the lawyer find out from Mr Guest? What did Mr Utterson believe?
8. ☐ What happened to Dr Lanyon a few weeks after he saw Dr Jekyll?
9. ☐ What did Mr Enfield find out about the laboratory?
10. ☐ Why do Poole and Mr Utterson break the door to the laboratory? Who, or what, did they find on the floor?
11. ☐ What did Dr Jekyll ask Dr Lanyon to do in his letter?
12. ☐ What did Dr Lanyon see that frightened him so much?

3 Viewpoints • Whose viewpoint do these sentences (1-6) come from?

a Mr Utterson
b Dr Lanyon
c Dr Jekyll

1. ☐ Dr Jekyll said something that was wicked.
2. ☐ Mr Hyde was a very bad man who did terrible things.
3. ☐ Mr Hyde was able to do what he wanted.
4. ☐ Mr Hyde was free from responsibility, but this came at a price.
5. ☐ The change from Mr Hyde to Dr Jekyll was shocking.
6. ☐ Henry Jekyll was a friend. Only he could tell his own story.

4 Characters • Who do the sentences (1-6) describe? You can use more than one character (a-f) for some sentences.

a Mr Utterson **b** Dr Lanyon **c** Dr Jekyll **d** Mr Hyde **e** Poole **f** Mr Enfield

1. ☐ He is honest and professional. He cares about his friends.
2. ☐ He is interested in mysteries, but he is respectful of others.
3. ☐ He is a good scientist. He doesn't always see other points of view.
4. ☐ He wants to do his own thing, but he feels bad when it hurts others.
5. ☐ He doesn't care about other people. He lives for his own pleasure.
6. ☐ He is loyal and a hard worker. He is worried about his employer.

5 Interpretation • In Chapter 1, we read that Mr Enfield and Mr Utterson aren't very similar. Is this true? What about Dr Lanyon and Dr Jekyll? Are they similar?

e.g. Mr Enfield and Mr Utterson can keep a secret. Dr Lanyon and Dr Jekyll have strong views about science.

6 Vocabulary • Unscramble the letters (a-l) using the clues (1-11).

0.	argue	**a**	uqrlrea	*quarrel*
1.	watched	**b**	okodle ta	....
2.	terrible	**c**	edualdrf	....
3.	enjoy	**d**	elki	....
4.	apparatus	**e**	uietqmpen	....
5.	story	**f**	eatl	....
6.	wicked	**g**	lvei	....
7.	solicitor	**h**	awlrey	....
8.	arrive (at)	**i**	ehrac	....
9.	trustworthy	**j**	toeshn	....
10.	real	**k**	retu	....
11.	inspected	**l**	xeianmde	....

THE CHARACTERS

1 Use the words in the box to make positive and negative adjectives to describe the characters.

curiosity → *He is curious.*
being open-minded → *He is <u>not</u> open-minded.*

....
....
....
....

....
....
....
....

....
....
....
....

....
....
....
....

responsibility • respectability • fairness • trust • loyalty • arrogance • violence • cruelty • curiosity • friendship • keeping secrets • being open-minded

THINK!

2 Which values and feelings do you think each chapter is about? Choose one or more words from the box above and complete the boxes below.

Chapters 1-2-3-4 ▸ ....

Chapters 5-6-7-8 ▸ ....

THE STORY

3 In the word cloud there is a list of feelings and themes. Which of these do you associate with *The Strange Case of Dr Jekyll and Mr Hyde*? Explain your answers and write them in the boxes.

curiosity anger
ambition fear
justice violence good
failure
respectability
kindness trust friendship
regret evil

Positive

....

....

....

Negative

....

....

....

Both

....

....

....

YOUR TURN!

4 What about you? Which feelings and values do you think matter the most? Now prepare your own word cloud using the words above. Make them big or small according to the importance they have for you. Add some of your own.

This reader uses the expansive reading approach: where reading is not only the enjoyment of the story and the discovery of a new language, but an opportunity to make cultural connections.
The new language introduced in this step of our **Reading & Training Life Skills** series is listed below and language from lower steps is included, too. For a complete list for all six steps, see *The Black Cat Graded Readers Handbook* at *blackcat-cideb.com*.

Step THREE B1.2

Verb tenses

Present Perfect Simple: unfinished past with *for* or *since* (duration form)
Past Perfect Simple: narrative

Verb forms and patterns

Regular verbs and all irregular verbs in current English
Causative: *have / get* + object + past participle
Reported questions and orders with *ask* and *tell*

Modal verbs

Would: hypothesis
Would rather: preference
Should (present and future reference): moral obligation
Ought to (present and future reference): moral obligation
Used to: past habits and states

Types of clause

2nd Conditional: *if* + past, *would(n't)*
Zero, 1st and 2nd conditionals with *unless*
Non-defining relative clauses with *who* and *where*
Clauses of result: *so; so ... that; such ... that*
Clauses of concession: *although, though*

Other

Comparison: (*not*) *as / so ... as*; (*not*) *... enough to; too ... to*

Step Three

If you enjoyed this reader, try another one in Step Three...

- *Jane Eyre*, by Charlotte Brontë (Life Skills)
- *The Canterville Ghost*, by Oscar Wilde (Life Skills)
- *The Time Machine*, by H.G. Wells

Step Four

...or take a step forward to Step Four!

- *Jack the Ripper*, by Peter Foreman
- *North and South*, by Elizabeth Gaskell (Life Skills)
- *Northanger Abbey*, by Jane Austen